The TRIUMPHANT RETURN OF BLACKBIRD FLYNT

Peter Ullian

BROADWAY PLAY PUBLISHING INC
New York
212 772-8334
BroadwayPlayPub.com

THE TRIUMPHANT RETURN OF BLACKBIRD FLYNT

First printing: December 2014
I S B N: 978-0-88145-615-8

Book design: Marie Donovan
Page make-up: Adobe Indesign
Typeface: Palatino
Printed and bound in the U S A

ABOUT THE AUTHOR

Peter Ullian's work for the stage has been produced off-Broadway, regionally, and internationally, and includes: HESTER STREET HIDEAWAY: A LOWER EAST SIDE LOVE STORY, produced off-Broadway by En Garde Arts; SIGNS OF LIFE (with lyrics by Len Schiff and music by Joel Derfner), produced off-Broadway by AMAS Musical Theatre, regionally at the Village Theatre and Victory Gardens, and internationally at Divadlo DISK in the Czech Republic; FLIGHT OF THE LAWNCHAIR MAN (with music and lyrics by Robert Lindsey-Nassif) directed by Harold Prince at the Prince Music Theater and the Ahmanson Theatre, and subsequently produced at Goodspeed Musicals and 37 Arts, as well as throughout the United States and in Liverpool and Edinburgh; ELIOT NESS IN CLEVELAND (with music and lyrics by Robert Lindsey-Nassif), produced at the Directors Company, the Denver Center Theatre Company, and the Cleveland Playhouse; THE TRIUMPHANT RETURN OF BLACKBIRD FLYNT, produced at the Cleveland Public Theatre and Vertigo Theatre Factory; BIG CONSPIRACY, produced at HOME for Contemporary Theatre and Art and the Café Voltaire; STUCK IN LUXEMBOURG, produced at Theatre Winter Haven; and BIG BOSSMAN, produced at the Cleveland Public Theatre, also published by B P P I. FLIGHT OF THE LAWNCHAIR MAN is published and licensed by Theatrical Rights Worldwide, and continues to be produced throughout the United States. The original cast recording of LAWNCHAIR MAN is available on the album *3hree* from DRG Records. Ullian's play NEW AMERICAN CENTURY was developed at the Lark Play Development Center and at 4th Wall at the Beacon. His play BLACK FIRE WHITE FIRE was presented at Jewish Plays Project's OPEN: The Festival of New Jewish Theater at the 14th Street Y, and his follow-up play, SPIRIT IN THE SKY, was developed at the Hollins Playwright's Lab and at Jewish Plays Project. His play DANCING NAKED IN THE LINE OF DUTY was developed at the American Theater Company. He wrote book and lyrics for the ten-minute musical THE DREAMS YOU CHOOSE (music by Scott Ramsburg), which premiered as part of the Mill Mountain Theatre's Overnight Sensations. His awards for dramatic writing include the Roger L Stevens Award from the Kennedy Center/A T & T Fund for New American Plays for IN THE SHADOW OF THE TERMINAL TOWER; two Gilman & Gonzalez-Falla Musical Theatre Foundation Commendation Awards; and two N E A production grants (FOR FLIGHT OF THE LAWNCHAIR MAN and SIGNS OF LIFE.) He also received a Barrymore Award Nomination for Outstanding New Play for FLIGHT OF THE LAWNCHAIR MAN. His screenplays include *Justice* (Paramount); *Denial* (Zeal Pictures); and *A Beginner's Guide to Armed Robbery* (Hollywood Pictures/Windancer Films). His original screenplay *Survivors* was optioned by Oscar-winning producer Mark Johnson, and subsequently optioned by actor Alfred Molina and director Mark Rydell. His fiction includes *Owen's Blood* (Cemetery Dance and Hardboiled), *The Vietnamization of Centauri V* (DAW Books anthology *Star Colonies),* and *Ribbons and Tin,* (Cemetery Dance, paper and ebook.). He is a contributor to *The Field Guide to Poetic Playwriting,* published by Rose Metal Press. He has taught creative writing at SUNY Old Westbury and playwriting at the M F A Hollins Playwrights Lab. He has been profiled in *Jewish Week, The Cedar Rapids Gazette,* the *Cleveland Plain Dealer,* and *The Los Angeles Times.* A member of the Dramatists Guild, he is a graduate of Oberlin College and the University of Iowa's Playwrights Workshop. He lives in the Hudson Valley with his wife and two children. He can be found on the web at peterullian.com.

THE TRIUMPHANT RETURN OF BLACKBIRD FLYNT was originally developed in workshop as part of the Cleveland Public Theatre's Fourth Festival of New Plays (Linda Eisenstein, Festival Director), and was produced by Artistic Director James A Levin. It was first presented on 12 September 1986. The cast and creative contributors were:

LADY JANE .... Palmar Hardy
THOMPSON .... Alec Rubin
CLOVIS .... Craig Strasshofer
MORGAN .... Alan Trethewey
BLACKBIRD FLYNT .... James A Levin

Director .... Linda Eisenstein
Light design .... Robert Stegmiller
Sound .... Earl Gottlieb

THE TRIUMPHANT RETURN OF BLACKBIRD FLYNT was first performed at the Cleveland Public Theatre, and was produced by Artistic Director James A Levin. It opened on 14 February 1987. The cast and creative contributors were:

LADY JANE.. Palmar Hardy
THOMPSON .... Rick Dahl
CLOVIS .... Craig Strasshofer
MORGAN.. Alan Babb
BLACKBIRD FLYNT .... James A Levin

Director .... Linda Eisenstein
Set & costume design....................................... Christine Sell
Light design .... Debra Mercedes Whitford

A subsequent revised version of THE TRIUMPHANT RETURN OF BLACKBIRD FLYNT was first performed at the Little Theater-Hall Annex at Oberlin College. It opened on 15 October 1987. The cast and creative contributors were:

LADY JANE..Kelly Kiyomi Caulk
THOMPSON...Tom Abernathy
CLOVIS...Charles Wurmfeld
MORGAN...Rich Kurshner
BLACKBIRD FLYNT ....Bill Walters

Director..James DePaul
Set design..Vincent G Fortunato
Light design ....Gregory D Cohen

THE TRIUMPHANT RETURN OF BLACKBIRD FLYNT was further revised for a production by Vertigo Theater Factory. It opened on 9 February 2002. The cast and creative contributors were:

LADY JANE.. Coralee Grebe
THOMPSON... Nicholas Dibble
CLOVIS... Eric Donaldson
MORGAN... Ben Hain
BLACKBIRD FLYNT... Ray Bills

Director	Rick Dahl
Assistant director	Debra Schumann
Light & sound design	Ben Hain, Eric Donaldson & Debra Schumann
Poster & program art	Jeffrey Johnson

This edition represents the author's definitive version of the play.

CHARACTERS & SETTING:

THOMPSON, *twenties, full of nervous energy and anxiety.*

LADY JANE, *early to mid-twenties. Although the youngest in the room, she has the most command, next to* BLACKBIRD. *Athletic, tough, sensible.*

MORGAN, *forty-ish, passionate, a bit wild, a bit gone to seed. An authentic relic of a more radical time.*

CLOVIS, *indeterminate age, alternates between hallucination and coma.*

BLACKBIRD FLYNT, *indeterminate age, although he's probably younger than* MORGAN *and older than* THOMPSON *and* LADY JANE. *Seemingly full of self-possession and control, guarded, extremely charismatic.*

It's possible for the characters to be played by actors of a variety of ethnicities. Although LADY JANE *makes references that would identify her as Jewish, she is also from the generation in which mixed-race and adopted Jews began to appear with more frequency, as well as the child of sixties radicals, so she could easily be biracial or non-white. This is not a requirement, but it's something to keep in mind when casting the play.*

Although it would be a stretch to describe LADY JANE *and* THOMPSON *as "punk rock" in their dress or attitude, it's worth noting that they derive their radical energy as much from that source as from sixties and seventies New Left radicalism, which they regard with a dash of suspicion.* BLACKBIRD FLYNT *appeals to them for the very reason that he seems to bridge the two, offering direction for punk rage and redirection for burned-out radical leftists.*

An abandoned warehouse or factory on the outskirts of the city.

Time: Late 1986

ACT ONE

(An abandoned factory or warehouse)

*(*LADY JANE *sits to the side of a large crate that functions as a table. An ashtray overflowing with cigarette butts stands in the center of the crate.* THOMPSON *paces around the stage.* CLOVIS, *eyes shut, very still, a bloody bandage around his head, lies in a corner. There are various packages and boxes around the stage.)*

(Silence)

LADY JANE: Thompson?

*(*THOMPSON *does not answer.)*

LADY JANE: Thompson.

THOMPSON: *(Still pacing)* What?

LADY JANE: You're pacing.

THOMPSON: *(Not listening)* Yeah. *(He continues to pace)*

LADY JANE: Thompson...

THOMPSON: What?

LADY JANE: Stop pacing. Please.

THOMPSON: Oh. Sorry. *(He stops. Pause)* I can't. *(He continues pacing.)*

LADY JANE: You're wearing a hole in the floor.

THOMPSON: This floor is very sturdy. This is a tough floor, Lady Jane. You do not need to worry about the condition of this floor. It will take more formidable stuff than the likes of me to put a hole in this floor, o.k? You could drive a…big truck…a tank…or something back and forth over this floor. If you wanted to. And not wear a hole in it.

LADY JANE: Thompson. Please. Sit down. You're going to tire yourself out. We need to conserve our energy.

THOMPSON: As soon as I feel tired, I'll sit down. Until then, I'll keep on pacing, if it's all the same to you.

LADY JANE: The idea behind conserving one's energy is that you do so in order to avoid feeling tired, and, since you mention it, it is not all the same to me, thank you very much. It's distracting.

THOMPSON: Distracting from what? What have you got to be distracted from? If I had something to be distracted from I wouldn't be pacing.

LADY JANE: I'm trying to think. You should try it sometime.

THOMPSON: What's that supposed to mean?

LADY JANE: What do you think it's supposed to mean?

THOMPSON: That I do not think.

LADY JANE: That's a reasonable interpretation.

THOMPSON: I think! I think deep thoughts! I just happen to do my best thinking when I'm pacing! Besides, if you were thinking hard enough you wouldn't be distracted!

LADY JANE: *(Getting up and pacing.)* I'm tired of thinking. I'll just pace instead.

(Beat)

THOMPSON: That's my thing.

LADY JANE: What is?

THOMPSON: Pacing.

LADY JANE: You invented it?

THOMPSON: No, but, I mean, it's my hallmark.

LADY JANE: Pacing is your hallmark?

THOMPSON: The hallmark of my individuality.

LADY JANE: Pacing?

THOMPSON: Yes.

LADY JANE: That's just the most pathetic thing I ever heard.

(Beat)

*(*THOMPSON *goes to sit, and think.)*

*(*LADY JANE *resumes pacing.)*

(After a moment, THOMPSON *springs up.)*

THOMPSON: Where is he?

LADY JANE: He'll be here.

THOMPSON: When?

LADY JANE: Soon.

THOMPSON: How soon?

LADY JANE: He said if anything went wrong, he'd meet us back here. Today.

THOMPSON: Well, anything kinda did go wrong, didn't it?

LADY JANE: Yes. It did.

THOMPSON: How do we know he'll show up at all? He couldn't seem to make it to the bank yesterday. What held him up then? How do we know he hasn't cut and run on us?

LADY JANE: Do you really believe that?

THOMPSON: I don't know what to believe! All I know is that this is one totally shitty state of affairs!

LADY JANE: He'll be here.

THOMPSON: He'd better. Or else.

LADY JANE: Or else what?

THOMPSON: I'm leaving.

LADY JANE: I'll miss you.

THOMPSON: You'll get over it.

LADY JANE: Eventually.

THOMPSON: Come with me.

(Beat)

LADY JANE: No.

(Beat)

THOMPSON: He can't expect us to wait around forever. They're gonna find this place sooner or later. Blackbird should know that.

LADY JANE: He does.

THOMPSON: He'd better. *(Beat)* Damn it, where is everybody? Six unaccounted for! Six! That's damn near, like, almost everybody! That is everybody, except for you and me and Clovis! They should have all been here, like, centuries ago.

LADY JANE: O K, O K, calm down…listen, anyone who made it out is going to have to lie extremely low. The city is crawling with cops and Feds by now. We tried to rob a bank. The authorities frown upon that kind of thing. Everyone's going to be looking for us, from cops on the beat to Ed Meese.

THOMPSON: *(To himself)* God, it stinks in here…it smells like…what does it smell like?

LADY JANE: Lemon.

THOMPSON: No, not lemon. Something stinkier. Like… fear…like…decay…like…mortality…like…cheese.

(Beat)

*(*CLOVIS *stirs and moans.)*

THOMPSON: Is he alright?

LADY JANE: I don't know. Check.

THOMPSON: Check what?

LADY JANE: If he's alright.

THOMPSON: How do I know if he's alright? I'm not a doctor.

LADY JANE: Make an educated guess.

*(*THOMPSON *goes to* CLOVIS *and kneels by him.)*

THOMPSON: He's breathing.

LADY JANE: That's a good sign.

THOMPSON: He looks sick though.

LADY JANE: That's not surprising.

THOMPSON: He's pale.

LADY JANE: He's lost a lot of blood.

THOMPSON: Oh, yuck.

LADY JANE: What?

THOMPSON: Is that his brain?

LADY JANE: Where?

THOMPSON: I think his brain is dripping out of his head.

LADY JANE: The whole thing?

THOMPSON: No, just part of it.

LADY JANE: How can you tell?

THOMPSON: I can't tell. I said I'm not a doctor.

LADY JANE: Well, thanks for clarifying that, because, you know, I wasn't totally sure whether you're really Trapper John, M D or not.

THOMPSON: I'm just guessing it's his brain, because it's dripping out of his head. What else do you keep in your head that could drip out like that?

LADY JANE: I don't know. Blood?

THOMPSON: Well, there's that too. And puss.

LADY JANE: Yuck.

THOMPSON: Should I try to put it back in?

LADY JANE: No! Don't touch it.

THOMPSON: We can't just let it drip out like that.

LADY JANE: Don't touch it.

(Beat. THOMPSON *moves closer to* CLOVIS.*)*

THOMPSON: Clovis? How ya' doing, Clovis? Can you hear me? It's me. Thompson. And Lady Jane. We're both here. Back…here. With you. *(Beat)* We got you out, Clovis. We picked you up and dragged you away. Put you back in the car. Brought you back here. We don't know what's happened to everyone else. They're not back yet.

(Beat)

LADY JANE: I don't think he can year you.

THOMPSON: Man, he looks sick.

LADY JANE: Well, his brain is dripping out of his head.

THOMPSON: I think he's dying. *(Beat)* We've gotta get him to a hospital of something.

LADY JANE: We can't. It's too dangerous.

THOMPSON: He could die.

LADY JANE: Maybe.

THOMPSON: He probably will.

LADY JANE: We don't know that.

THOMPSON: He could die right now!

LADY JANE: Then it won't make any difference if he dies in a hospital or here, will it?

THOMPSON: You're a cold hearted woman, you know that, Lady Jane?

LADY JANE: They're out there, Thompson. They are out there looking for us. They could be right outside, right now.

THOMPSON: You mean... *(Whispering)* ...they could be right outside this very second?

LADY JANE: That's exactly what I mean.

THOMPSON: *(Pause. Then, whispering)* What if they hear us?

LADY JANE: They won't. The floor is sturdy and the walls are thick.

THOMPSON: What if they drop a bomb on us like they did to the MOVE house in Philadelphia last year?

LADY JANE: Well, hopefully they won't, you know, because that worked out so well for everyone.

THOMPSON: *(He looks at* CLOVIS*, again.)* It was stupid to take him with us. We can't help him. He's never gonna be the same again, you know. You saw it. You were there. Bam! Finished. A bullet right in his brain. Like Gene Hackman in *Bonnie and Clyde.* He's gone. Comatose. No longer among the living. He's out of the picture. A complete blank. What the hell happened anyway? He was supposed to wait in the car. Why was he across the street?

LADY JANE: No way to tell.

THOMPSON: He wasn't even armed!

LADY JANE: The cops don't care about that.

THOMPSON: My head hurts. *(Beat)* Will you rub my temples?

LADY JANE: If you put that gun down.

THOMPSON: *(Looks at the gun, then to* LADY JANE*)* No. This gun stays with me at all times. It never leaves my side.

LADY JANE: Thompson, you never handled a gun for more than an hour at a time until yesterday. And now you won't let go of it.

THOMPSON: I have too handled a gun before. I always carry a gun.

LADY JANE: You never carry a gun.

THOMPSON: Well, I do now.

(Beat)

LADY JANE: At least holster the damn thing. Then I'll rub your temples.

*(*THOMPSON *puts the gun away in a holster or a pocket, goes to* LADY JANE, *sits with his back to her. She rubs his temples. He lights a cigarette.)*

LADY JANE: You're tense.

THOMPSON: No shit I'm tense. This is a tense type of deal.

LADY JANE: You've got to learn to redirect your energy. Tension is misdirected energy. You've got to learn to channel it. Control it.

THOMPSON: Aren't you tense?

LADY JANE: Of course I'm tense. But you're on the verge of panic.

THOMPSON: I am not on the verge of panic!

LADY JANE: No, you're right. You passed panic about an hour ago.

(Pause. LADY JANE *continues to rub* THOMPSON*'s temples.)*

THOMPSON: Everything is blown up. Everything is ruined. Our cover is blown. Our organization is a shambles. Our ideals have been compromised. Blackbird could be dead. Or in jail. Or both. What are we gonna do without Blackbird? What if we are the only ones left, Jane? You and me. And Clovis. What are we going to do then?

(Beat)

LADY JANE: *(Slowly)* Blackbird is not dead. Or in jail. Or Both. He will be here. Soon.

THOMPSON: He'd better.

(Beat. LADY JANE *rubs* THOMPSON*'s temples. Suddenly, there is a loud knocking at the door. He springs up and pulls out his pistol. She stands.)*

THOMPSON: What's that?

(Knocking again)

LADY JANE: The door.

THOMPSON: I can tell it's the door! Who is it?

LADY JANE: What, I have X-ray vision? I don't know.

(Knocking again)

THOMPSON: Blackbird?

LADY JANE: Maybe.

THOMPSON: One of the others?

LADY JANE: Also a possibility.

(Knocking again)

THOMPSON: Police?

LADY JANE: I don't know.

THOMPSON: What should we do?

(Knocking again)

LADY JANE: See.

THOMPSON: See?

LADY JANE: Who it is.

(Pause. More knocking)

*(*LADY JANE *and* THOMPSON *go to the door and stand on either side of it. His pistol is at the ready, she remains unarmed.)*

THOMPSON: Should I open it?

LADY JANE: Ask who it is first. Real casual.

THOMPSON: *(To door, and none to casual)* Who is it?

MORGAN: *(From behind the door)* Me!

THOMPSON: Morgan?

MORGAN: No, it's Alexander Haig!

THOMPSON: *(To* LADY JANE*)* It's Morgan.

LADY JANE: Thank God.

THOMPSON: What if it's not really Morgan?

LADY JANE: Thompson. It's not Alexander Haig.

THOMPSON: But how do we know it's really Morgan?

LADY JANE: It sounds like Morgan.

THOMPSON: What does Morgan sound like?

LADY JANE: Like Morgan.

THOMPSON: *(Indicating door)* Is that what Morgan sounds like?

LADY JANE: More or less.

MORGAN: Will someone open the door, please?

THOMPSON: Kinda gruff and throaty like that, right?

LADY JANE: Exactly. Gruff and throaty.

THOMPSON: But not that gruff and throaty.

LADY JANE: Well. He's probably tired.

THOMPSON: What if he's not alone?

LADY JANE: You mean like what if he brought the cops?

THOMPSON: Exactly!

LADY JANE: Would Morgan do that?

THOMPSON: I don't know. I mean, how well do we really know Morgan?

LADY JANE: Blackbird chose him. Blackbird trusted him.

THOMPSON: The cops could be holding him at gunpoint. You said they could be right outside!

MORGAN: *(Off)* Are you planning to let me in or shall I stay in a motel this evening?

THOMPSON: Morgan! Are you alone?

MORGAN: Yes!

THOMPSON: No cops with you?

MORGAN: No!

THOMPSON: Any in the general vicinity?

MORGAN: No! *(Beat)* Would you like me to get one?

THOMPSON: *(To* LADY JANE*)* If the cops are holding him at gunpoint, he might not be able to tell us the truth.

LADY JANE: You know what? Sometimes you just have to take a leap of faith.

*(*THOMPSON *opens the door.* MORGAN *enters and stands in the doorway, glaring.)*

THOMPSON: Morgan! What happened?

MORGAN: Gimmie.

*(*MORGAN *takes the cigarette from* THOMPSON'*s mouth and places it in his own, then sits at the table, his elbow on the table, his head resting in his hand, his cigarette between*

the fingers of the same hand. THOMPSON *looks at him for a moment of indecision, then lights a new cigarette.)*

(There is a short pause.)

MORGAN: *(Referring to the cigarette)* You slobbered all over it.

(There is another short pause. Then THOMPSON *gives his new cigarette to* MORGAN *and takes back his old one.)*

MORGAN: And I am NOT gruff and throaty.

LADY JANE: What happened, Morgan? Give us a report.

MORGAN: We didn't stand a chance. They cut everyone down. There were bullets coming out of the walls. Right out of the Goddamn linoleum. Cops and soldiers, everywhere...fucking shooting at us with real bullets... Everyone in the place had a machine gun. There were old ladies and children shooting at us. We were barely through the door when they cut us down.

THOMPSON: What about the others? Did any of the others get out?

MORGAN: You really are an asshole, Thompson, you know that?

THOMPSON: I'm not an asshole. Why am I an asshole? What did I do? Lady Jane, why's he calling me an asshole?

LADY JANE: What happened to Piñero?

MORGAN: I couldn't see. They must have got him, he was in the front.

LADY JANE: Wilson?

MORGAN: Dead.

LADY JANE: O'Neil?

MORGAN: Dead.

LADY JANE: Miller?

MORGAN: I couldn't see. Dead, I presume. Maybe captured. I don't know.

THOMPSON: Shit.

MORGAN: Asshole.

THOMPSON: He's doing it again!

LADY JANE: How did you get away?

MORGAN: Give me another cigarette.

(Slight pause. MORGAN*'s first cigarette is not done yet, but* THOMPSON *gives him a new one anyway.* MORGAN *lights the new one off of the old one.)*

THOMPSON: How did you get away, Morgan?

MORGAN: *(With a bitter, amused laugh)* Goddamn, you are a prick, Thompson, yes you are.

LADY JANE: Will you answer the question, Morgan?

MORGAN: I ran.

THOMPSON: You ran?

MORGAN: Fuck you.

THOMPSON: He ran.

MORGAN: Fuck you sideways.

THOMPSON: I can't believe you ran.

MORGAN: Fuck you upside down and inside out.

LADY JANE: Tell us what happened.

MORGAN: I ran. Across the street. Into a building. Up the stairs. Out the window. Up the fire escape. Over the rooftops. I saw everybody fall and I ran. I dropped my gun and I ran. I ran as fast as my little feet could take me. Piñero yelled "Run!" and I ran. He saw that it was hopeless and he tried to get us out. He would have run too, but he didn't get the chance. Bravery is not synonymous with stupidity, Thompson. So I ran. I ran into the street. There were cops everywhere. I ran for the first door I saw. Inside and up the stairs faster than I would have thought humanly possible, ten or twenty cops right on my heels. I'd be dead now, right now, dead or in jail or both if not for Blackbird.

THOMPSON: Blackbird? Where was Blackbird?

MORGAN: Oh, shut up, asshole...

LADY JANE: Morgan, where was Blackbird?

MORGAN: Second floor, Blackbird. I turned a corner and he grabbed me, out of nowhere, these hands come out of nowhere and grab me. I thought I was finished, I thought it was a cop. But the hands that grabbed me were not a cop's hands but the hands of that dear old boy, your friend and mine, our fearless leader, Blackbird Flynt. I was indeed surprised, and grateful, although more surprised than grateful, as the full ramifications of this incident were not, as yet, entirely clear to me. The next thing I knew, Blackbird threw me into a room and told me to take the fire escape to the roof. Then he went out to find the cops.

LADY JANE: To do what with the cops?

MORGAN: To find them. I know. It was suicidal. He said he'd "detain" them while I made my getaway, and out the door he went. There was nothing I could do.

THOMPSON: He said he'd detain the ten to twenty cops for you?

MORGAN: Yes. For me. Wasn't that sweet of him? He would have done the same for even you, Thompson.

THOMPSON: Great! Terrific! Bravery is not synonymous with stupidity, Morgan? Well, Blackbird had a bad case of both! Shit, shit, shit! This certainly changes things...

LADY JANE: Thompson, please. Morgan, you didn't see Blackbird again?

MORGAN: No. Not a sign of him. I spent the rest of the day and all night hopping from roof to roof, hiding in alleys, in garbage cans, and avoiding cops. And they were everywhere. Everywhere I turned there they were, hanging around in packs in front of drug stores, with automatic rifles in their big, greasy hands. I thought I was in an occupied country. And of course I was.

LADY JANE: How did you get all the way out here?

MORGAN: I walked and hid and walked and hid and walked. I hid more than I walked. There were roadblocks all over. It was slow going. Twenty-four hours of the finest fun and excitement. And guess what the speculation is on the radio? They think we're the remainders of the Weather Underground!

LADY JANE: No!

MORGAN: Yes!

THOMPSON: That sucks! We're not those left-over leftie losers who robbed that armored truck in Nanuet! We're an authentic anarcho-communal revolutionary vanguard! *(Beat)* Right?

LADY JANE: Close enough.

(Beat)

THOMPSON: Well. Where do we go from here, my coconspirators? Last of the Mohicans? Last of the Dogmen. We'll never see Blackbird again, you know. We won't. Blackbird's dead or in prison or both or who knows what. I know it. So do you. Which means we're all on our own now.

MORGAN: For Christsake, will you shut your great big drooling mouth already?

(Beat)

THOMPSON: Do you have something to get off your chest, Morgan? Is there some reason for your unfriendliness? For this vehemence, which I cannot help but notice is directed exclusively towards me? I mean, what have I done? Have I made fun of your family? Insulted your honor? Offended your sensibilities? Forgive me if I misread the situation, Morgan, but I can't help but sense that the vibes you're sending in my direction are somewhat less than exuberant. So what is the deal, Morgan?

MORGAN: *(Casually)* You are such a little bitch, Thompson.

THOMPSON: *(Finally angry)* That's enough, Morgan! Now, what is it with you? Answer me! I don't have to take this shit from you, you know! I'm second in command, and don't you forget it!

MORGAN: No you're not! Piñero is second in command!

THOMPSON: Do you see Piñero anywhere, Morgan? Do you? He's not here. He's probably dead, according to you. He's certainly in no position to fulfill his duties as second in command. Which means said duties now fall on my shoulders! Mine! Not yours, but mine!

MORGAN: Wrong! Said duties now fall on Lady Jane's shoulders! Lady Jane is now our second in command!

(Beat)

THOMPSON: *(To* LADY JANE*)* Is that true?

LADY JANE: It pretty much is, yeah. I was pretty much second in command even when Piñero was still around, actually.

MORGAN: See? Lady Jane outranks you.

(Beat)

THOMPSON: It doesn't matter. I'm still way above you Morgan, regardless. I am definitely higher up on the chain of command than you are.

MORGAN: Fuck you.

THOMPSON: That's enough of that, Morgan!

MORGAN: Fuck you twice.

THOMPSON: I could have you shot!

*(*MORGAN *bursts into laughter.)*

LADY JANE: Where do you two think we are?

*(*MORGAN*'s laughter abates. Beat.)*

LADY JANE: We do not have the time for this. This is serious business, robbing banks and undermining the Government. We're trying to start a revolution, here. And we can't do it with the two of you behaving like a couple of spoiled children.

THOMPSON: We can't do it now regardless! We have no organization and no Blackbird and the F B I is due on our doorstep at any minute! And you know what they do! Shoot first, identify the bodies later! Remember 6221 Osage Avenue? Fred Hampton? Attica? 1466 East 54th Street? Kent State?

MORGAN: *I* remember that stuff, Thompson! You weren't even born when most of that stuff happened!

THOMPSON: I remember the siege at 1466 East 54th Street! I remember when they bombed the MOVE house on Osage Avenue in Philly!

MORGAN: Well, of course you remember Osage Avenue, that was like a year ago! I remember when they assassinated Fred Hampton! What were you then, two? Do you have the slightest idea of what we're talking about?

THOMPSON: I don't have to prove my authentic anarcho-communal revolutionary vanguardian credentials to you!

LADY JANE: Can we possibly just deal with the situation at hand instead of debating who has the bigger anarcho-communal revolutionary vanguardian credentials?

(Beat)

THOMPSON: Any suggestions?

LADY JANE: For a start, we can stop fighting and start thinking.

(They do. Beat)

THOMPSON: It won't matter. We're finished. We're finished without Blackbird. Even if we could get out of here, then what? Just set up shop somewhere new? It's not as simple as that. We have no direction without Blackbird. No leadership. We've already begun to dissolve. We're useless without him.

(Beat)

LADY JANE: Blackbird is not dead.

THOMPSON: No, he's merely getting the third degree from J Edgar Hoover. Tied to a chair. A desk lamp two inches from his face.

LADY JANE: He's not in jail either.

THOMPSON: Right…

LADY JANE: He's not.

THOMPSON: Of course he is.

LADY JANE: No. He's not.

THOMPSON: How would you know?

LADY JANE: I know.

THOMPSON: What, you called up a psychic and asked? I hope you only spoke to a certified psychic from the American Psychic Association.

LADY JANE: Think about it...do you really believe a couple of cops could take down Blackbird?

MORGAN: Those were not a couple of cops! Those were a shitload of cops! A whole ton of cops! A great big bunch of cops!

LADY JANE: I'm not worried.

(Beat)

MORGAN: Me neither.

(Beat)

THOMPSON: I am.

LADY JANE: You're too tense, Thompson.

THOMPSON: We've established that.

LADY JANE: You need to relax.

MORGAN: He needs to shut up.

LADY JANE: That's enough, Morgan.

MORGAN: Yes, Ma'am.

LADY JANE: You're a bit on the tense side yourself.

MORGAN: Yes, Ma'am.

LADY JANE: You could also do with a bit of relaxation.

MORGAN: Whatever you say, Ma'am.

LADY JANE: Are you mocking me? Because I'll kick your ass all over this room if I think you're mocking me, Morgan.

(Beat. MORGAN *is silent.)*

MORGAN: O K. Let's do something constructive. I agree.

LADY JANE: Good.

MORGAN: Do you know what I'd like to do?

THOMPSON: No.

MORGAN: Shave!

THOMPSON: What?

MORGAN: Shave! Let's shave!

LADY JANE: Morgan...

MORGAN: Just you and me, Thompson. Let's shave. Together. Let's have a shaving contest! Who can shave the fastest and bleed the least! What do you say, Thompson old buddy of mine?

LADY JANE: Morgan...

MORGAN: Don't worry, Jane. Don't worry about us. We can handle it. *(Goes to* THOMPSON*)* We can handle it, can't we, Thompson, old buddy of mine? *(Puts his arm around* THOMPSON*'s shoulders)* Of course we can, old buddy old pal. Confidant. Comrade in Arms. Cohort. Constant source of inspiration. Wellspring of good will. This is kid's stuff, Jane. We went through the war together, Thompson and me. Don't forget that. If we could handle that, we can handle anything.

LADY JANE: Morgan, you and Thompson did not fight together in any war.

MORGAN: That's where you are mistaken, Lady Jane. Me and Thompson here certainly did fight together. Side by side. Nam. Sixty eight. The jungles of Southeast Asia. We went through the war. Straight on through and out the other side. Jesus, what a time. Wasn't that a time, Thompson? Wasn't that a time? A time to try the souls of men. Wasn't that a time.

LADY JANE: I bet you went to Canada in '68.

MORGAN: Is Canada in Southeast Asia? 'Cause that's where I was in '68. With Thompson.

LADY JANE: Thompson was a kid in '68.

MORGAN: We were all just kids, Lady Jane. All of us. All-American kids about to get a hard lesson in geopolitics.

THOMPSON: I was in Operation Urgent Fury.

(Beat)

LADY JANE: You invaded Grenada?

THOMPSON: I was nineteen.

LADY JANE: Is that true?

THOMPSON: I was a Marine.

(Beat)

MORGAN: You were a Marine?

THOMPSON: Yeah.

MORGAN: Fuck off.

THOMPSON: I was.

MORGAN: Get out of here.

THOMPSON: Can't. No where to go.

(Beat)

MORGAN: See, Lady Jane. I told you Thompson and me could handle it. What do you say, Thompson? We already know who's the better man. Let's see who's the better shaver.

(Beat)

THOMPSON: You're out of control, Morgan. You're completely out of control.

MORGAN: Yes, but will you accept my challenge?

THOMPSON: You're a lunatic. You're a babbling idiot.

MORGAN: YES! But will you join me in a little game of Shave?

THOMPSON: Why?

MORGAN: Because it's a grand idea.

THOMPSON: Get away from me.

MORGAN: Come on, Thompson! Think of it! The cool blade of your disposable razor against your cheek! The smell of shaving cream! The roar of the water! Is it not a grand scenario I put before you?

THOMPSON: No!

MORGAN: Come on, Thompson! Where is you sense of adventure?

THOMPSON: Go away!

MORGAN: Where's your sense of camaraderie? Miller and I used to shave together all the time.

THOMPSON: Then go shave with Miller!

MORGAN: I can't, Thompson. You know that. Miller is not available. So, you'll have to do.

THOMPSON: Leave me alone!

MORGAN: In my opinion…

THOMPSON: I don't give a shit about your opinion! You have gone completely out of your head! You are psychotic! Your opinion does not merit earnest consideration at this time!

MORGAN: Now that's not necessarily fair, Thompson…

THOMPSON: Your opinion is not valid!

MORGAN: But what about yours, Thompson? It's your opinion I'm interested in! What is your opinion on the matter, Thompson?

THOMPSON: My opinion is that you are an idiot!

MORGAN: But that doesn't answer my question, Thompson! Wrong opinion! Now, WILL YOU OR

WILL YOU NOT JOIN ME IN A LITTLE SHAVING CONTEST?

THOMPSON: NO! I WILL NOT!

(Beat)

MORGAN: Fine! I'll shave by myself.

*(*MORGAN *exits through the bathroom door. Sound of water rushing out of a faucet. He returns with a bowl of water, a towel, a small mirror, a can of shaving cream and a disposable razor. He sits in the chair he previously occupied and commences shaving.* THOMPSON *watches him for a moment, then exits to the bathroom and returns with his own towel and razor. He sits in another nearby chair.* MORGAN, *without any sign of emotion, positions the bowl and mirror so they can both use it.* THOMPSON *commences shaving.)*

MORGAN: I've got a head start.

THOMPSON: I'm not racing with you. I need a shave, that's all.

MORGAN: All right. O K. We won't have a shaving contest. We'll have a party. A shaving party! What'd'you say, Jane. We don't want to be exclusive or anything. Let's all have a shaving party! C'mon. Join us. You can shave your legs. Or your armpits. Whichever needs it most.

LADY JANE: Morgan, I don't feel like shaving.

MORGAN: Of course you do, Jane. That's what we all feel like right now. A good shave. Scrape off all our stubble. Make ourselves presentable. Clean ourselves up. Clean up our act. Face the new day with a new face...or new armpits. Make a fresh start. It'll become a trend. Clean-shaven revolutionaries. Perfumed radicals. Smooth-legged feminists.

LADY JANE: Morgan, if you want me to shave my legs, you'll have to take my pants off.

MORGAN: I'm serious. What we all need is a good cleaning up party. C'mon, Jane. Join the party. Get with the program. Follow the party line. Even Blackbird Flynt needs a shave now and then.

LADY JANE: That's all right, Morgan. You and Thompson go ahead and shave.

MORGAN: O.K. Fine. Thompson— Commence shaving. Lady Jane will come around.

(They continue shaving.)

(After a moment, LADY JANE *goes into the bathroom and returns with a razor and a towel. She approaches them.)*

*(*LADY JANE *drops her pants.)*

(Unsettled, MORGAN *nicks himself.)*

MORGAN: Ow.

THOMPSON: I win.

MORGAN: We're not having a contest! We're having a party.

*(*LADY JANE *begins to shave her legs.)*

LADY JANE: I was naked when I met Blackbird.

(Unsettled, THOMPSON *nicks himself.)*

THOMPSON: Shit!

MORGAN: Ha!

LADY JANE: I was born a revolutionary. I know we're not supposed to talk about our pasts—we were newly reborn the day we signed up with Blackbird and our pasts are forgotten—but I'll let you in on a little secret—my parents were actual, radical, bomb-throwing yippie, Weather Underground refugees. They went on a bombing spree of government institutions back in the day. I was just a kid. A love child. My parents went into hiding after the bombings. I grew up shuffling from safe house to safe house, changing names, assuming new identities. Weird thing for a kid. Got to be I didn't know what my original name was. Still don't. But eventually, my parents hid in plain sight, and we became totally squaresville—picket fence, two car garage, the whole *megilla*h. I even became a Bat Mitzvah. But, you know, in High School, I started to rebel. Drugs, boys, girls, trouble. My parents tried private education, but that didn't help. And after I'd been kicked out of three boarding schools, gone through my obligatory substance abusing phase, my obligatory lesbian phase, and my obligatory punk rock phase, I came home and found my parents gone. They just picked up stakes and left town, taking up new identities somewhere else—but I had no idea where. I guess they thought the Feds were closing in, or maybe I was making too much of spectacle of myself and they got scared I was going to blow their cover. So, I was alone. I lived on the streets, got involved with an anarchist collective, and made a furtive stab at various misdirected terroristic activities that were closer to vandalism than serious political actions. Emulating my parents, I guess, but badly. Eventually, I wound up on a commune in Oregon. It was actually a pretty cool place. I got clean there, got healthy, got my shit together. But, of course, I was a dumb kid, and one day, I looked around and all I could see was shattered, disappointed fugitive hippies grasping for an idealized past that was gone, gone, gone. I looked around and I began to feel sick. I looked around at all these people. And I realized I hated them. I despised them. These people around me, these people I'd been spending all my time with, they were what was making my stomach turn. Why should I hate these people, I wondered. What have they ever done to me? I mean, they basically saved my life. But then I realized: I hated them for their ineffectuality. These people had all made a stab at change, in some cases a violent stab, in some cases non-violent, in both cases, maybe a naïve stab at change, but then they had retreated, retreated to these communes, these safehouses, these underground Utopias. These people were fairly bright human beings. People who maybe, just maybe, could have made a difference. But they had withdrawn. They'd just given up the ghost. They had abandoned the struggle. They no longer had the courage to get up off their asses and do something. Anything. The smallest little thing. They might as well have been in Siberia for all the good they were doing. They'd exiled themselves to this unreal, insular place, and they were eating wild rice and lentils. That really pissed me off. I mean, it shouldn't have pissed me off, because those wild rice and lentils nourished me and these people took me off the streets. But I guess these people made me think of my parents, who bailed on me. And I had all that punk rage in me, that I'd tried to channel into street anarchism, but that was politically a totally unfocussed rage. I was a stupid kid. A high school drop out. Still a teenager. What did I know?

And while I was thinking this, looking at all these people, I suddenly saw, for the very first time, Blackbird Flynt. He was on his recruitment tour, the same one during which he picked up our whole team. But I was his first recruit.

Blackbird stood out. He looked more like Marlon Brando than Jerry Rubin…young Marlon Brando. Maybe a little Velvet Underground-era Lou Reed, but taller and without the druggyness. Definitely a soupcon of Joe Strummer. A dash of Dylan just before the motorcycle accident. Jack Reed in Red Square. Lord Byron without the limp.

He was standing by a picnic table, wearing a black leather jacket, a white scarf tossed back over one shoulder, black jeans and black leather boots. His dark hair hanging down over one eye. And eating black olives. Black organic olives. Just popping one olive after another into his mouth, with a motion cool and exact. And he was watching. Watching everything all at once with this amazing intensity, that was so alive, so genuine, so unlike everyone and everything around him. There was something about the way he held himself, so relaxed and still so full of exploding energy. And the way he ate those olives. As if each olive had to be eaten exactly at the time he ate it and not a second sooner or a second later. As if each olive was an essential olive. I thought he was the only person around who wasn't going to waste.

Blackbird looked at me then. I'd been swimming and I was naked, which was pretty normal, we all went swimming naked, it was a commune, after all. I was rising from the small lake at the edge of the compound, and he looked at me, not sexually, but with an understanding that the girl rising from the water was like an amorphous thing that he could mold into a new being. My nakedness seemed oddly appropriate, symbolic. Because it was like I was being born all over again, emerging naked and new into the world, starting all over again. And I was. That day, I was born again.

Blackbird understands action. He believes in change. And that is a big achievement. Just to believe in change. He's not self-satisfied. He's not static. Society's great machine lumbers along, leaving discouraged radicals along the industrial highway like so much roadkill but there is Blackbird to give this nation a sharp kick in the groin whenever he can. He's not a relic or an imitator of the sixties and seventies radical left. He's a brand new movement. Maybe he won't change much. Or one day he may bring it all crashing down. But he will not accept exile. He will do his damnedest to break free and to help others break free. And that is something. That is something worth doing.

(Pause)

(They have finished shaving.)

LADY JANE: I won the shaving contest, by the way.

THOMPSON: We're not competing. We're partying.

(They return the various articles to the bathroom. LADY JANE *puts her pants back on.* THOMPSON *lights a cigarette.* MORGAN *takes out rolling papers and begins to roll a joint.)*

MORGAN: Anyone care to join me?

LADY JANE: Morgan...

THOMPSON: *(Slowly)* Is that...pot?

MORGAN: No, it's cow dung.

THOMPSON: You can't smoke that!

MORGAN: You're right. It's not cow dung.

THOMPSON: You can't smoke it!

MORGAN: Yes I can. I've practiced.

THOMPSON: You can't smoke it at this time, Morgan.

MORGAN: Why not? Will I explode?

THOMPSON: Morgan!

MORGAN: Thompson...this ganga, this reefer, this Mary Jane, this grass, this shit, this pot was presented to me as a gift by none other than our dear departed Piñero. I am smoking it in his honor.

THOMPSON: Revolution is a serious business! One cannot smoke pot at critical moments and remain a successful revolutionary! I mean, that was the whole problem with your generation!

MORGAN: What do you know about my generation? You don't even know anything about *your* generation.

THOMPSON: I know the Weather Underground blew up their own Greenwich Village Townhouse because somebody was trying to smoke a joint and assemble bombs at the same time!

MORGAN: You don't know that! Nobody knows why those bombs exploded!

THOMPSON: We need to keep our minds clear and our reflexes sharp! Particularly now, with our whole organization in shambles, we cannot afford to sit back, relax, and light up a joint!

MORGAN: The Revolution is dead, Thompson. It breathed its last gasp yesterday morning, rolled over on its belly and died. We made a stab at it, but we can't keep it alive. These are not revolutionary times, Thompson. We should have figured that out when Ronald Reagan was re-elected. We've failed.

THOMPSON: Don't give me shit about revolutionary times! You don't sit on your ass and wait for revolutionary times! You make revolution! As long as there is poverty and oppression, you have revolutionary times! Maybe everybody out there has been anesthetized out of their skulls by the Gipper and his rambling tales of cities on hills and driving down the P C H, but that's why we've got to keep it up! To wake people up and make them realize they've got a choice! But we can't do that if we sit back, relax, and light up a joint! A joint does not the road to revolution make!

MORGAN: You're kidding yourself, Thompson. The Revolution's out of commission. There are better things to do with one's time. This is one of them. *(He lights his joint.)*

LADY JANE: *(To* MORGAN*)* Thompson's right.

THOMPSON: Ha!

LADY JANE: We can't afford this kind of distraction. We've got work to do. The Revolution is not dead as long as there are people left to fight for it.

MORGAN: Sorry, Jane. But I'm tapped right the fuck out. And now I want to smoke a joint.

(Beat)

THOMPSON: God, I want a drink...

MORGAN: Ha!

THOMPSON: But I'm not going to, Morgan! I'm not going to drink! I have a bottle, but I'm not going to open it! Because I know my responsibilities, Morgan! And because I still believe in the revolution!

MORGAN: Glad to hear it, Thompson. What bottle?

THOMPSON: What?

MORGAN: What bottle? A bottle of what?

(Beat)

THOMPSON: *(Sheepishly)* Peach schnapps.

MORGAN: Pussy!

LADY JANE: Morgan. I don't think Blackbird would approve.

MORGAN: I'm sure he wouldn't. Blackbird never drank peach schnapps in his life.

LADY JANE: I'm talking about your controlled substance-abuse, Morgan.

MORGAN: Please, Jane. I have been running and hiding for nearly twenty-four hours. I have inched my way over miles of inhospitable terrain at an extremely excruciating pace. I have hid for hours beneath piles of garbage in the hopes of avoiding certain people trying very hard to kill my ass, or at least hurt me very badly. Forgive my rudeness, but if I want to get stoned, that's my business. I deserve it.

(Beat)

CLOVIS: HUNDREDS!

*(*MORGAN *jumps out of his seat,* CLOVIS *mumbles incoherently.)*

THOMPSON: He spoke…

MORGAN: Jesus! I didn't even see him there! What in hell happened to him?

THOMPSON: Got a bullet in his brain—

LADY JANE: It grazed his skull.

THOMPSON: What are you talking about? It went in his brain.

MORGAN: Shit! And he's talking?

LADY JANE: Well, he wasn't until now…

THOMPSON: You can't talk with a bullet in your brain. It impedes the speech.

LADY JANE: It grazed his skull, for God's sake!

THOMPSON: His brain is dripping out of his skull!

LADY JANE: You don't know it's his brain! It could be… puss!

MORGAN: Yuck.

THOMPSON: You're an optimist, Lady Jane.

MORGAN: Well, how'd it happen? I thought he was supposed to wait in the car.

LADY JANE: He was.

MORGAN: They shot him in the car?

LADY JANE: He wasn't in the car. He was across the street.

MORGAN: Well, what was he doing across the street?

LADY JANE: Who knows?

MORGAN: Jesus…

THOMPSON: He's kinda like…getting shot like that… kinda like a martyr…to the Revolution…sort of?

CLOVIS: Hundreds and hundreds and more…I saw… hundreds…

MORGAN: I think he's trying to tell us something.

THOMPSON: What could he be trying to tell us?

MORGAN: I don't know.

(Beat)

THOMPSON: Find out.

MORGAN: You find out.

THOMPSON: You find out.

MORGAN: You.

THOMPSON: No.

MORGAN: Why not?

THOMPSON: I don't feel like it.

MORGAN: You're scared.

THOMPSON: No.

MORGAN: Yes you are.

THOMPSON: No I'm not.

MORGAN: Yes you are.

THOMPSON: So are you.

(Beat)

LADY JANE: For God's sake… *(She goes to* CLOVIS.*)* Clovis? Can you hear me?

CLOVIS: *(Eyes still shut)* No…can't hear a word… only yesterday…I saw…hundreds…yesterday…I remember yesterday…I have a past…therefore I am…I think…Now he tells me! I saw…yesterday I…I came to a conclusion, yesterday…I say…I understood… something…I had not understood before…for the very first time…Recently it's begun to dawn on me…a certain previously murky terrain has suddenly come to light… Blinding light! And no one there to see! What a dilemma! So rich in knowledge and yet…I saw…I see…but cannot say…talked to Blackbird yesterday… he told me to…for a while… *(He trails off incoherently.)*

*(*LADY JANE *tends to* CLOVIS *as he calms down.)*

MORGAN: You know, he really doesn't look very good.

THOMPSON: Of course he doesn't! People do not look good when they have a piece of lead inside their skulls!

MORGAN: Oh shut up.

THOMPSON: I've had must about enough of you, Morgan!

MORGAN: I've had more than enough of you…

THOMPSON: Listen—

MORGAN: No! No listening! I've done enough listening! There's nothing to listen to anymore. Nothing left that's worth the effort of opening up your ears. Nothing but cross currents of bullshit and a vague stench of…is that cheese? Our senses are on overload. Let's give them a break. I'm tired of it. There's nothing left to say, Thompson. So let's not say it. Let the world go on by itself. Let it make as much noise as it wants. Let's just have some silence, Thompson. Some peaceful, relaxing silence.

(A silence)

*(*LADY JANE *leaves* CLOVIS, *who is more or less still again, and goes to the table.* MORGAN *and* THOMPSON *look at each other for a moment. Then* MORGAN *goes to the table*

and retakes his seat. THOMPSON *looks at* MORGAN. *He looks at* LADY JANE. *Both are looking away, at the table or floor, tired and avoiding eye contact with their comrades.* THOMPSON *turns and looks at* CLOVIS, *who seems to be sleeping. He goes to him, kneels beside him and looks closer.)*

THOMPSON: *(Pause. Then loudly, definitively, as he gets up.)* Stand up, everybody! We're going to storm the Bastille!

MORGAN: Oh, for Christ's sake...

THOMPSON: Shut up, Morgan! We're not finished yet! We had a job to do that we left unfinished! And now we're going to finish it!

LADY JANE: You're not serious, are you?

THOMPSON: Damn straight! I'm tired of sitting on my ass waiting for Blackbird. I'm going back to that bank and I'm going to get something accomplished.

LADY JANE: Accomplished? What exactly do you think you'll get accomplished?

THOMPSON: That's what I intend to find out.

MORGAN: Stupid...there are patrols out all over the place. You won't get half a mile from here. Even if you make it to the bank, they'll gun you down as soon as you show your face.

THOMPSON: I'll give it a try.

MORGAN: We already tried! We failed! Accept it!

THOMPSON: Acceptance is not an option.

MORGAN: Jesus Christ...

LADY JANE: This is foolishness, you know.

THOMPSON: I don't care what it is. I'm doing it. With or without your help.

*(*THOMPSON *finds the gun box and empties the contents on the floor. There are a few pistols and some ammunition.)*

MORGAN: Not much is it?

THOMPSON: It'll do.

(THOMPSON *begins to load the revolvers.)*

LADY JANE: Don't try to be a martyr, Thompson. It won't get you anywhere.

THOMPSON: I am not trying to be a martyr. I am trying to rob an bank.

LADY JANE: But it amounts to the same thing. You'll die and our cause will not have been furthered by even a tiny little bit.

THOMPSON: We'll see about that.

LADY JANE: We don't need any more martyrs, Thompson. We've got enough of them already. More martyrs do not the Revolution make.

THOMPSON: Martyrdom is not the issue.

LADY JANE: What is the issue then?

THOMPSON: The Bastille.

LADY JANE: For God's sake, Thompson, do you want to wind up like Clovis? Do you want a bullet of your own in your brain? Is that it? Is that the status quo now? Is that how Revolutionaries keep up with the Joneses? Let's all go out and put bullets in our brains? Clovis was...is a great guy, Thompson, but let's not get carried away! If you want to emulate your friend, there are better ways to do it!

THOMPSON: I thought you said that the bullet only grazed his skull?

LADY JANE: *(Trying to be patient)* I did.

THOMPSON: Well, did it or didn't it?

LADY JANE: *(Still trying to be patient)* It did.

THOMPSON: So? I can handle that!

LADY JANE: *(No longer patient)* Thompson, a bullet grazing one's skull is not exactly a condition worth striving for! And I can tell you right now that you will not have Clovis' relative good luck!

THOMPSON: That's not what I meant! I meant...I mean...never mind!

LADY JANE: Damnit, Thompson, is this your fucked up idea of heroism? Can't you understand that the Alamo was just not that heroic!

THOMPSON: What?

LADY JANE: Custer's Last Stand is not a handbook for dealing with tense situations!

THOMPSON: Custer wasn't at the Alamo.

LADY JANE: *(Still trying to be patient)* I know that, Thompson.

THOMPSON: Custer's Last Stand was much later.

LADY JANE: *(Still trying to be patient)* I know that, Thompson.

THOMPSON: And it was at Little Bighorn.

LADY JANE: *(Still trying to be patient)* I know that too, Thompson.

THOMPSON: So, what are we talking about, Custer or Davy Crockett?

LADY JANE: Thompson...

THOMPSON: Or Jim Bowie?

LADY JANE: *(About to lose her patience, and with a look to* MORGAN.*)* You really are an asshole, Thompson.

MORGAN: Ha!

THOMPSON: Don't be tense, Jane. There's nothing to be tense about. I'm not doing this to make you tense. Would you like me to rub your temples?

LADY JANE: Christ, if you have to kill yourself, don't go to all this trouble! Just pick up this gun and put a bullet through your thick skull! It's so much easier! Really, it's very, very easy. Just blast a hole through your head. In one side and out the other. Shoot your brains out all over the wall. We'll clean it up. Don't worry. Go ahead. If that's what you want, go ahead and do it!

THOMPSON: Jane, I think you're being mean.

LADY JANE: After the mess we've seen at the bank, why do you want to go back and make another one? I'll tell you what's going to happen, Thompson. I'll tell you exactly what's going to happen. You are going to walk in through the door and you are going to feel a bullet rip through your right arm. And it is going to feel like fire. And then you are going to feel the same thing in your left arm. And you will look at your arms, and you will see blood and bone and muscle and flesh hanging out of the holes in your sleeves. And then you are going to catch one in the gut, and it is going to hurt like nothing you have ever felt before. And then you are going to feel your leg, your whole right leg get shot out from under you by a shotgun blast and go flying across the room. And you will go down. You will be on one knee and one stub. And all you will see is the floor, and the pool of blood, getting wider and wider. Your blood. Your own crimson, scarlet, all-American, ruby-red blood. And you won't be able to move, because every muscle in your body has a bullet lodged inside of it. You won't be able to breathe, because there will be bullets in both of your lungs. And then an F B I man in a brown suit and dark glasses is going to walk up to you, put a pistol to the back of your neck, and blow your moronic brains out all over the floor.

(Beat)

THOMPSON: Now you're really being mean, Lady Jane.

LADY JANE: Is that what you want, Thompson? Your brains spread out all over the floor of the bank? Our little hideout's not a good enough place to deposit your insides? Is that it? Is that what you want? A dramatic place to expire? Is that what you want?

THOMPSON: No.

LADY JANE: WELL, WHAT THEN?!?

(Beat)

MORGAN: Oh, let him kill himself if he wants to.

THOMPSON: Thank you, Morgan. *(Beat. He continues to load the pistols.)*

MORGAN: Look, Thompson, this really isn't necessary you know.

THOMPSON: It is for me.

MORGAN: Why? To prove you're brave? We know you're brave. You pulled Clovis off the street and put him back in the car, right? I thought you must have. I knew Jane must have been the one providing cover, because she's a better shot than you. But you are just as brave. You're braver than me, I know that. I ran. You don't need to go around proving you're brave.

THOMPSON: It's nothing to do with that.

MORGAN: What then?

THOMPSON: I just have to do something decisive. Waiting around here, it's…it's like death. Only not as decisive. This way, if I die…well, at least I'll know it's for real. But here, sitting waiting…we don't exist. And I don't like that.

(Beat)

MORGAN: I'm sorry I was nasty, Thompson.

THOMPSON: That's all right, Morgan. *(He goes back to the revolvers.)*

MORGAN: I was just letting off steam. It wasn't personal.

THOMPSON: I know.

MORGAN: You're not really an asshole.

THOMPSON: Thanks.

(Beat)

MORGAN: Thompson, please don't do this! I don't want you to die.

THOMPSON: Thank you, Morgan. That's very sweet of you.

MORGAN: I'm serious.

THOMPSON: Yes. *(He begins to load himself up with revolvers in his pockets, belt, etc.)*

MORGAN: Look...I like you, Thompson. I really do. It would grieve me to see you killed.

THOMPSON: You're a good guy, Morgan. You really are. I wish you well.

MORGAN: Blackbird wouldn't do this, you know.

THOMPSON: I know. *(He heads toward the door.)*

MORGAN: NO!

*(*MORGAN *rushes to the door and stands in front of it, barring* THOMPSON'*s way.)*

MORGAN: I won't let you do this, Thompson. I won't let you kill yourself for no good reason.

THOMPSON: And if I had a good reason?

MORGAN: Then I might.

*(*MORGAN *and* THOMPSON *laugh. The laughter subsides.)*

THOMPSON: Let me by, Morgan.

MORGAN: No.

THOMPSON: Please.

MORGAN: No.

THOMPSON: I really don't want to tussle with you.

MORGAN: I'm not letting you go.

THOMPSON: I'm stronger than you.

MORGAN: You're not, actually.

THOMPSON: I'm younger than you.

(He is.)

MORGAN: So?

THOMPSON: You're old and creaky and arthritic. One push and you'll crumble and topple over.

MORGAN: Age-ist.

THOMPSON: Hippie.

MORGAN: Anarchist.

THOMPSON: Yippie.

MORGAN: Punk.

THOMPSON: Red diaper baby.

(Beat)

MORGAN: You take that back.

THOMPSON: Not on your life. Get out of my way.

(Beat)

MORGAN: Not on your life.

(Beat)

THOMPSON: We're going to have to tussle then.

MORGAN: So it seems.

THOMPSON: You won't hold a grudge if I hurt you?

MORGAN: You're not going to hurt me. I might hurt you.

THOMPSON: If you do, I'll forgive you before I even hit the ground.

MORGAN: That's very understanding of you.

THOMPSON: But you won't hurt me, old man.

MORGAN: Let's find out.

(Beat)

THOMPSON: Ready?

MORGAN: Yes.

(Beat. They tussle. They are not gentle, but they try not to hurt one another. THOMPSON *finally manages to slip away and rushes towards the door.* MORGAN *immediately springs up and goes after* THOMPSON. *Just before he reaches him,* THOMPSON *flings the door open.* BLACKBIRD *is standing in the doorway. He looks exactly as described by* LADY JANE, *minus the olives. All are frozen. Pause)*

BLACKBIRD: May I come in?

END OF ACT ONE

ACT TWO

(The action is continuous from the end of ACT ONE. All are in the same positions.)

BLACKBIRD: May I come in?

(MORGAN *and* THOMPSON *move to let him in.)*

BLACKBIRD: Thank you. *(He looks around, then casually drops a bag by the table.)* Well. Fine mess we've gotten ourselves into, eh?

THOMPSON: Blackbird?

BLACKBIRD: You look remarkably clean-shaven this morning, Thompson. *(He looks at* MORGAN.*)* And so do you, Morgan. What's the occasion?

THOMPSON: We'd given up hope—

MORGAN: He thought you were dead—

THOMPSON: Or in jail—

MORGAN: Or both.

BLACKBIRD: So you decided to break out the shaving equipment and clean your faces in my memory. How nice.

LADY JANE: Blackbird...

BLACKBIRD: *(Smiling)* Hello, Jane. *(Beat)* Well, comrades. I'm back.

MORGAN: But...

BLACKBIRD: Yes?

MORGAN: The cops…ten…twenty of them…how…?

BLACKBIRD: Six cops, Morgan. Only six.

MORGAN: But how…is it you're…not completely dead?

BLACKBIRD: Well, it was not a simple matter, I can assure you.

MORGAN: No…I bet it wasn't…

BLACKBIRD: No. You see, after I left you, I ran down the hallway, turned the corner at the top of the stairs and Bam! Six machine guns pointing right in my face. For a moment I felt quite dumbfounded, even a trifle… intimidated.

THOMPSON: And…?

BLACKBIRD: I smiled.

MORGAN: You smiled?

BLACKBIRD: I smiled.

MORGAN: He smiled!

THOMPSON: You didn't really smile?

BLACKBIRD: I'm afraid I did.

THOMPSON: Jesus Fucking Christ! He smiled!

LADY JANE: A small or a large smile?

BLACKBIRD: Oh, somewhere in between. Just a simple, strong, amicable smile.

LADY JANE: And what did the police do?

BLACKBIRD: They just stared at me.

THOMPSON: So what did you do?

BLACKBIRD: I asked, "Can I help you?"

MORGAN: You didn't!

BLACKBIRD: I did.

THOMPSON: You are a maniac, Blackbird!

BLACKBIRD: Far be it from me to argue with you.

MORGAN: So what did they do?

BLACKBIRD: *(To* MORGAN*)* They asked me if I'd seen a man who looked like you. And then one of them inquired as to whether I'd just tried to rob a bank. I said no, of course. Then they asked me my name.

(Beat)

LADY JANE: What did you tell them?

BLACKBIRD: I said I was Cecil Beaton.

THOMPSON: Who?

MORGAN: He's an actor.

THOMPSON: What?

MORGAN: An actor.

THOMPSON: Who?

MORGAN: Cecil Beaton.

THOMPSON: Cecil Beaton is an actor?

MORGAN: Was an actor. He's dead.

THOMPSON: Was an actor.

MORGAN: He was in *Mutiny on the Bounty.*

THOMPSON: And now he's dead.

MORGAN: Yes.

THOMPSON: Oh.

LADY JANE: Shut up! Blackbird, what happened next?

BLACKBIRD: They asked for identification.

THOMPSON: Oh no.

BLACKBIRD: Oh yes.

MORGAN: Did you have any?

BLACKBIRD: Certainly none that identified me as Cecil Beaton.

MORGAN: What did you do?

BLACKBIRD: I told them so.

MORGAN: Oh no...

BLACKBIRD: Then they began to suspect.

THOMPSON: Oh no.

BLACKBIRD: So they pushed me up against the wall...

MORGAN: Oh shit...

BLACKBIRD: And searched me.

THOMPSON: Oh boy...

LADY JANE: Did they find anything?

BLACKBIRD: Nothing but a pack of cigarettes and a zippo lighter.

THOMPSON: Good.

BLACKBIRD: Although they failed to return either one.

THOMPSON: Oh. Would you like one of mine?

BLACKBIRD: Yes please, if you have one to spare.

THOMPSON: Yes, of course.

*(*THOMPSON *gives* BLACKBIRD *a cigarette and lights it. Pause as* BLACKBIRD *takes a deep drag and exhales.)*

MORGAN: So then what?

THOMPSON: Yes, then what?

BLACKBIRD: Well, they debated as to what to do with me.

THOMPSON: What to do with you?

BLACKBIRD: Arrest me, let me go, shoot me etcetera.

MORGAN: Yeah?

BLACKBIRD: All the while with my face shoved into the wall and my hands on my head.

MORGAN: Bastards...

THOMPSON: So? What did they decide?

BLACKBIRD: Well, they almost let me go.

MORGAN: Almost?

BLACKBIRD: Well, they stopped rubbing my face in the wall.

THOMPSON: That was nice of them.

BLACKBIRD: But then one of them suddenly remembered that they were supposed to take in all suspects and suspicious types, like myself.

MORGAN: Sounds grim.

BLACKBIRD: It gets grimmer. Someone realized that I fit a description of the alleged leader of the alleged organization that allegedly had just attempted to hold up the bank that was allegedly across the street.

THOMPSON: Shit. That is grim.

BLACKBIRD: So they pushed my face back up against the wall.

MORGAN: Sounds intimidating.

BLACKBIRD: It almost was.

LADY JANE: Did they handcuff you?

BLACKBIRD: They were about to.

THOMPSON: And...?

BLACKBIRD: I pushed them.

THOMPSON: You what?

BLACKBIRD: I pushed them.

MORGAN: You pushed them?

BLACKBIRD: I threw myself backwards and pushed them away. One of them fell. Three were off balance. The others went for their guns. *(Pause. He takes a deep drag on his cigarette.)*

THOMPSON: So, what did you do?!?

BLACKBIRD: I killed them.

(Pause)

LADY JANE: What?

BLACKBIRD: I killed them.

MORGAN: All of them?

BLACKBIRD: Yes.

MORGAN: All eight of them?

BLACKBIRD: All six of them. There were only six.

MORGAN: For Christ's sake, how?

BLACKBIRD: As I pushed them back, I snatched a machine gun.

THOMPSON: You snatched a machine gun? Just like that?

BLACKBIRD: He wasn't holding onto it very firmly. And once I had it, I commenced firing. It wasn't very pretty, but it seemed the only alternative. I dropped them and took off.

(Pause)

THOMPSON: You did not.

BLACKBIRD: I did not what?

THOMPSON: You did not kill six heavily armed policemen all at once at point blank range.

BLACKBIRD: They were not being as attentive as they should have been, and four of them were off balance.

THOMPSON: It's not possible.

BLACKBIRD: That's what I thought at first. But I decided it was worth a try.

THOMPSON: It is simply not humanly possible.

BLACKBIRD: But it is, Thompson. I wouldn't be here if it weren't.

THOMPSON: You really killed six cops all at once?

BLACKBIRD: A machine gun fires very quickly.

(Pause)

MORGAN: You saved my life, Blackbird. Thank you very much.

BLACKBIRD: The pleasure is mine, Morgan. I just wish I could have done something for the rest of our team.

(Pause)

THOMPSON: What kind of a machine gun was it?

BLACKBIRD: Pardon?

THOMPSON: I'm just wondering. Most of them were carrying M-16s. Further evidence of the militarization of our urban police forces.

LADY JANE: Then it was probably an M-16, Thompson. Isn't that right, Blackbird?

BLACKBIRD: It most certainly was.

(Beat)

LADY JANE: That's a lot of dead cops.

BLACKBIRD: Yes.

LADY JANE: That's regrettable.

BLACKBIRD: Yes. Cops are the proletariat, even if they serve the Master's Death Machine. That's why we never call them "pigs". What I did is nothing to celebrate. But it was unavoidable.

THOMPSON: Collateral damage.

MORGAN: Don't use that phrase. "Collateral damage." That's a fascist phrase.

LADY JANE: How did you happen to be in that building, Blackbird? We expected to see you in the bank.

BLACKBIRD: I expected to see myself there as well. I woke up yesterday morning to the sound of my door being kicked in. I just had time to slip out the window before they got through. I spent hours trying to contact you and get to the rendezvous. I had to hide in all sorts of inhospitable locations. Police everywhere. By the time I got to the bank, it was too late. It had already started. *(Beat)* It would seem we were betrayed.

(Pause)

THOMPSON: Who?

BLACKBIRD: I don't know.

THOMPSON: You don't think it's one of us?

(Beat)

BLACKBIRD: I don't know. *(Beat)* What happened to Clovis?

LADY JANE: Bullet grazed his skull—

THOMPSON: *(Simultaneously:)* Bullet in his brain—

BLACKBIRD: I see. Has he been conscious?

LADY JANE: Semi.

BLACKBIRD: I see.

LADY JANE: Is there anything we can do for him?

(Beat)

BLACKBIRD: We'll have to see. Is this everybody, then? We're the last?

LADY JANE: I think so. I don't see how anyone else could have made it.

BLACKBIRD: Well then, this is it. *(He takes four pistols out of a bag and lays them out on the table.)*

LADY JANE: What have you got there, Blackbird?

BLACKBIRD: A few souvenirs of my experience with the metropolitan police. Thompson?

THOMPSON: Yes?

BLACKBIRD: Check our weapon and ammunition reserves, Thompson.

THOMPSON: I already did, Blackbird.

BLACKBIRD: Check them again.

THOMPSON: O K. *(He does.)*

BLACKBIRD: Morgan?

MORGAN: Yes?

BLACKBIRD: Have you already checked the provisions?

MORGAN: Not yet!

BLACKBIRD: Do so.

MORGAN: Yes sir! *(He does so.)*

BLACKBIRD: Jane?

LADY JANE: Yes?

BLACKBIRD: Rub my temples, if you would be so kind. *(Beat)* Do you think that's sexist?

LADY JANE: What, that you asked me to rub your temples instead of check on the ammunition?

BLACKBIRD: It's just that Morgan and Thompson are so inelegant when it comes to the art of therapeutic touch.

LADY JANE: It's not sexist. *(She rubs his temples.)* We were worried about you, Blackbird.

BLACKBIRD: You didn't think I'd make it?

LADY JANE: I knew you would. But we were still worried. It's nice to have you back.

BLACKBIRD: Believe me—the pleasure is all mine.

LADY JANE: You must have wondered.

BLACKBIRD: Wondered about what?

LADY JANE: If you'd make it.

BLACKBIRD: I wondered about a lot of things, Jane.

LADY JANE: I can imagine. *(Beat)* We've got a lot of work to do.

BLACKBIRD: Yes. We do.

*(*THOMPSON *is finished with the guns in the gun box and is about to go check the guns on the table.)*

BLACKBIRD: DON'T TOUCH THAT!

(Beat. Everyone looks at BLACKBIRD.*)*

THOMPSON: I thought you wanted me to check all our ammunition?

BLACKBIRD: That isn't our ammunition. It's mine.

THOMPSON: Oh.

BLACKBIRD: I don't want you to touch a single one of those pistols.

THOMPSON: O K.

BLACKBIRD: Understand?

THOMPSON: Yes.

BLACKBIRD: Good.

THOMPSON: I'm sorry.

BLACKBIRD: That's all right.

THOMPSON: We're good, otherwise. I mean, we don't have enough guns for an extended siege, but we've got pistols and ammo for each of us. Even if Clovis recovers.

BLACKBIRD: Good. Morgan?

MORGAN: Uhhh...we've got enough food and supplies for about a week.

BLACKBIRD: Good.

LADY JANE: Can we wait a week, Blackbird?

BLACKBIRD: Why can't we?

LADY JANE: Well, what are the chances they'll find this place by then? Especially if someone tipped them off.

BLACKBIRD: A good question.

LADY JANE: I mean, I think we can assume they don't know about this location yet, or else they'd already be here.

BLACKBIRD: Why is that, I wonder?

LADY JANE: That they don't know about this place?

BLACKBIRD: Yes.

LADY JANE: Because who ever tipped them off doesn't know about this place?

BLACKBIRD: Or because whoever tipped them off hasn't told them about this place.

LADY JANE: Why would the person who tipped them off not have told them about this place if they knew about this place?

BLACKBIRD: A good question. Perhaps because that person is dead. Or, here.

LADY JANE: Why would the person who tipped them off come back here?

BLACKBIRD: A good question.

(Beat)

LADY JANE: If the person who tipped them off isn't here but is instead someone who didn't know about this place, who could that person be?

BLACKBIRD: In that case, not one of us. But someone who found out key information *from* one of us. Because one of us confided or confessed or bragged to a sexual conquest or a confidant whom he or she shouldn't have, and told them too much. But not everything.

LADY JANE: Not this location.

BLACKBIRD: Precisely, Nancy Drew.

(Beat)

LADY JANE: So, that doesn't really narrow anything down very much.

BLACKBIRD: No. *(Beat)* I'm sorry I snapped at you, Thompson.

THOMPSON: It was my fault.

BLACKBIRD: True.

(Beat)

THOMPSON: Well, what now, Blackbird?

BLACKBIRD: That's the question.

THOMPSON: Oh. I thought you'd have a plan…

BLACKBIRD: Of course you did.

(Beat)

*(*THOMPSON *starts unloading his other pistols and replacing them in the gun box.)*

MORGAN: You really were going to storm the Bastille, weren't you, Thompson?

THOMPSON: Yes.

MORGAN: But now you don't have to.

THOMPSON: Now I don't think I really want to. *(Beat)* Who was he, again?

MORGAN: Who?

THOMPSON: Cecil Beaton.

MORGAN: I told you! An actor!

THOMPSON: Who was in *Mutiny on the Bounty*? Who'd he play?

MORGAN: Captain Bligh.

THOMPSON: Oh. Oh! I know who you're talking about! He was also in *Hunchback of Notre Dame*!

MORGAN: Right! And *Witness for the Prosecution*! And, he directed that movie with Robert Mitchum!

THOMPSON: Which one? *Cape Fear*?

MORGAN: No...

THOMPSON: *El Dorado*?

MORGAN: With John Wayne?

THOMPSON: And James Caan.

MORGAN: No, not that one.

THOMPSON: Which one then?

MORGAN: The one where Mitchum plays an evil minister with "love" tatooed on one hand and "hate" tattooed on the other.

THOMPSON: *Night of the Hunter! Night of the Hunter!*

MORGAN: That's the one, that's the one!

THOMPSON: Cool! *(Beat. He thinks, intensely. Then, realization:)* That was Charles Laughton, you moron.

MORGAN: What?

THOMPSON: You're thinking of Charles Laughton!

(Beat)

MORGAN: Oh. *(Beat)* Then who the fuck is Cecil Beaton?

(Beat)

LADY JANE: Is anyone hungry?

BLACKBIRD: No.

MORGAN: Me neither.

THOMPSON: Me neither.

LADY JANE: Me neither.

(Beat)

MORGAN: *(Getting up and walking around)* Well. I'm feeling better. I must say, I am really feeling better.

THOMPSON: *(Unconvincingly:)* Good.

MORGAN: Yes sir. I am feeling good. I mean, I am really feeling good.

*(*MORGAN *is standing over* BLACKBIRD*, who is sitting, thinking. He stands there, silently, for a few moments.)*

BLACKBIRD: Can I help you?

MORGAN: Uhhh…no.

BLACKBIRD: Good.

MORGAN: *(Moving away from* BLACKBIRD*)* Yes sir. I feel like I could run a mile.

LADY JANE: You've never run a mile in your life.

MORGAN: No, but I've crawled a mile. I've crawled ten miles. Over broken glass and barbed wire. Actually, I was a jock in high school.

THOMPSON: Everyone was a jock in high school.

MORGAN: You weren't.

THOMPSON: Fuck you.

MORGAN: All right, what'd you do?

THOMPSON: *(Beat)* Gymnastics.

MORGAN: Get outta here!

THOMPSON: I did.

MORGAN: You're full of it, Thompson.

THOMPSON: Balance beam.

MORGAN: Ha!

THOMPSON: Rings.

MORGAN: Ha!

THOMPSON: Pommel horse.

MORGAN: Ha!

THOMPSON: Double back flips.

MORGAN: Double ha!

THOMPSON: Springboard.

MORGAN: Triple ha!

THOMPSON: Fuck you.

LADY JANE: I hated jocks in high school.

MORGAN: You were a debutante in high school, that's what you were!

LADY JANE: I was not! I was underground! There are no debutantes underground!

MORGAN: You said you were trying to fit in with fake identities! I bet you were more square than Ozzie and Harriet.

LADY JANE: Yeah, but I was a rebel.

MORGAN: But before you were a rebel, you were a debutante. You have to have something to rebel against, after all.

LADY JANE: There are no Jewish debutantes.

MORGAN: Oh yes there are! There are Jewish debutante balls!

LADY JANE: I was not a debutante.

MORGAN: You were too. I used to chase little girls like you around the playground.

LADY JANE: In high school?

MORGAN: No. In high school I did something else with them.

LADY JANE: You're a pig.

MORGAN: Damn straight. Damn! I am feeling fine. I'll tell you, Blackbird, I was really worried that we'd never see you again.

BLACKBIRD: So was I.

MORGAN: I thought you'd never come back.

BLACKBIRD: Did you think I'd let you wait around here forever?

THOMPSON: We wouldn't have waited around here forever.

BLACKBIRD: You wouldn't have?

THOMPSON: No. Not forever.

BLACKBIRD: Are you sure?

THOMPSON: Sure.

BLACKBIRD: Are you absolutely sure?

THOMPSON: Sure.

BLACKBIRD: Are you absolutely, positively sure?

(Beat)

THOMPSON: No.

BLACKBIRD: You might have?

(Beat)

THOMPSON: Maybe.

BLACKBIRD: You might have waited?

THOMPSON: Possibly.

BLACKBIRD: You might have waited forever?

THOMPSON: Conceivably.

BLACKBIRD: Forever?

THOMPSON: Maybe.

BLACKBIRD: For little old me?

THOMPSON: Yeah.

BLACKBIRD: Forever is a long time, Thompson.

THOMPSON: Yeah. I'm beginning to figure that out. And it just keeps getting longer.

(Beat)

MORGAN: Don't be so gloomy, Thompson. Things are looking up. Blackbird's back. We're a family again.

THOMPSON: A smaller family.

MORGAN: All right, a smaller family. But we will make it.

THOMPSON: I hope you're right.

MORGAN: Sure I'm right. We'll set up shop somewhere new.

THOMPSON: Just like that? Start again?

MORGAN: Sure. Won't we, Lady Jane?

LADY JANE: Of course we will.

THOMPSON: Where?

MORGAN: Doesn't matter.

THOMPSON: Yes, it does. We can't just set up shop anywhere.

MORGAN: Sure we can!

LADY JANE: We'll set up wherever we think we'll be most useful, where we think we're most needed, and where we think our efforts will be most fruitful. C'mon, Thompson. Have a little faith. Blackbird's gotten us this far, hasn't he? Things are bleak, I know. I'm not forgetting about all our fallen comrades. But, and I don't mean to be cruel about it, this is a rough road we've chosen. A really rough road.

THOMPSON: It's very rough.

LADY JANE: It is. It's very rough. No one's denying that. But every one of us knew what we were signing up for. You don't jump ship at the first sign of bad weather.

THOMPSON: You're mixing metaphors. And this isn't bad weather. This is a fucking iceberg, and we're the Titanic.

LADY JANE: But we've made it to the lifeboats, Thompson, don't you get it? And there are oceans full of possibilities in every direction.

THOMPSON: Lady Jane, you are a very nice person, but when it comes to metaphor, you are a sadistic torturer.

LADY JANE: Nothing's over until it's over, Thompson. And we are not over. We've made it this far. We'll make it the rest of the way.

THOMPSON: When?

MORGAN: Why are you so Goddamn time-oriented? There are more important things than time, y'know! We're not on any kind of deadline or anything. We got time. Plenty of time. All we got is time.

THOMPSON: Lady Jane said they'll find this place sooner or later.

MORGAN: But not right away, Thompson, because if they already knew they'd already be here, so we've got time.

THOMPSON: Not too much time.

MORGAN: Well, some time.

LADY JANE: We've got more than time, Thompson. We've got each other.

THOMPSON: I guess we'll see.

LADY JANE: You will see. You will see exactly what I mean.

MORGAN: You remember the time you got thrown in jail, Thompson? When they caught you packing heat, even if it was only a starter's pistol? Remember that? Who got you out? Remember?

THOMPSON: Yes.

MORGAN: Who?

THOMPSON: Blackbird Flynt.

MORGAN: That's right. That's exactly right. Blackbird Flynt. He walked right in there in a three-piece suit and pretended to be your lawyer. Remember that? And he scared the shit out of those cops. They thought they were gonna get their butts sued. He had them thinking that they'd violated every Goddamn constitutional article in the Bill of Rights, and a few that hadn't even been adopted yet. And you were out walking around in an hour's time. Remember that?

THOMPSON: I remember.

MORGAN: Good. *(Inspired:)* Blackbird's given us...a reason. I mean...at one time, I used to think at one time that there was nothing worth doing anymore. Everything had been done. And it hadn't worked. I used to think that there was nothing left in life but pure, hedonistic pleasure. Art, books, philosophy, religion...they were all an old ticket to me. So, after I was other-than-honorably-discharged, I rode around in a Ford convertible and drank. Drank Jack Daniels. Fucked around. A lot. But then one day I took a swig of J D and it tasted different. Didn't go down as smooth. I'm looking around at what I'm doing, it's O K, it's fun, I'm spending a lot of energy, I'm driving fast, I'm getting drunk, I'm feeling good. But I'm bored. Because there's nothing else for me to do. And that didn't seem right. In fact, that seemed wrong. If all the world's got to offer me is whiskey and cars, which are great, I mean I like whiskey and cars, they're fine—but if that's all there is...then something is definitely wrong. And I thought, maybe if I took all this energy and redirected it, maybe I could try to rearrange the world, instead of just rearranging my brain cells. Well, I wasn't going to run for office. So I decided to subvert. I decided to attack. Whatever I could find to attack. I decided that was the only road to progress. Attack. Take the other route. Take the underground route. So I began to harass the local police station with crank phone calls. Ordered pizza and shit like that. Well, they got used to me, they hung up. I was young, Thompson, younger than even you, and almost as dumb. Well, maybe not that dumb. The point is, before you attack you've got to have something more, you've got to have a target, you've got to have a plan, you've got to have a vision, you've got to have a reason for your revolution. I didn't have those things. I needed to find someone who did. I didn't have anybody. I was lonely. A lonely revolutionary. So, I went to the movies. Looking for somebody. Somebody to inspire me. And I found myself identifying, not with the hero, not with the anti-hero, not even with the number one bad-guy, but with the cheap, slimy hood who does all the dirty work and gets killed about a half an hour before the end of the film. I saw myself as Vic Morrow. It wasn't that I wanted to get killed, it was just that I saw myself in that function, but not working for Sydney Greenstreet or anybody like that, but working for the hero. The man with the vision. The hero and his henchman. The hero never had a henchman. He had a sidekick, but never a henchman. The hero never had a cheap, slimy hood to do all his dirty work. And I just couldn't get it out of my head how much better off we'd all be if he did. *(Beat)* You always wanted to be the hero, didn't you, Blackbird?

(Beat)

BLACKBIRD: I don't believe in heroes. History is not the story of great men.

MORGAN: And the fact that you believe that—that's what makes you a hero, in my book. *(To everyone:)* It took me a while. I followed a lot of false Gods, dead-end ideologies, violent radical organizations with no real sense of purpose, stale, misdirected motivations, rebels without a clue. I fell back into despair and whiskey on more than one occasion. But eventually I found what I was looking for. Someone to be a henchman for. When I thought I was completely burned out and truly lost, I found Blackbird. Or he found me. *(Beat)* Blackbird's my Elvis. I just want to hand him his guitar. *(Beat)* How about you, Thompson? Where do you fit into this picture?

THOMPSON: I dunno…

MORGAN: Sure you do, Thompson. You wouldn't be here if you didn't know.

THOMPSON: Well…

MORGAN: Yeah?

THOMPSON: Well, I, sorta…

MORGAN: C'mon, Thompson, spit it out…

THOMPSON: Well, I always, sorta wanted to be…Elvis… too.

(Beat)

MORGAN: What?

THOMPSON: I always sorta wanted to be Elvis, too.

MORGAN: You wanted to be Elvis?

THOMPSON: Sure.

MORGAN: You really wanted to be Elvis?

THOMPSON: Doesn't everybody?

MORGAN: NO. I mean, everybody identifies with Elvis. That's why he's Elvis. But there's only one Elvis, Thompson. There can't be two Elvises. One Elvis. Only one. And everybody has to realize that.

THOMPSON: What about Tom Jones?

MORGAN: What?

THOMPSON: Tom Jones was sort of like Elvis and they were around the same time.

MORGAN: They never made a movie together, though, or play a show together, did they? Because there can only be one Elvis at a time.

THOMPSON: What about Prince?

MORGAN: What?

THOMPSON: Prince. He's sort of like Elvis, now.

MORGAN: Fucking Prince? OhMyGod, what is the matter with you? I mean, I see myself for what I am. What the hell do you see yourself for?

THOMPSON: I see myself for what I could be.

MORGAN: For what you could be? You really think that by any stretch of the imagination, by any possible… anything, in total opposition to every law of gravity and physics, that you could ever be Elvis?

THOMPSON: Stranger things have happened.

MORGAN: No. A stranger thing has never happened. And never will. Aren't you satisfied, Thompson?

THOMPSON: Well…I mean…I'm not unsatisfied, it's just that—

MORGAN: When you're part of a machine, Thompson, when you're part of a machine, and you're just a small little spigot in that machine, if you go around wanting to be the guy running that machine, do you know what happens, Thompson? Do you?

THOMPSON: What?

MORGAN: The machine fucks up, Thompson, that's what happens! Springs and gears and belts go breaking and flying off in all directions!

THOMPSON: I haven't fucked up the machine.

MORGAN: Oh no? Oh no? What about fifteen minutes ago, Thompson, when you were all fired up to storm the Goddamn Bastille? You don't call that fucking up the machine?

THOMPSON: No.

MORGAN: What do you call it, then?

THOMPSON: Well, I mean we had no Elvis then, we had no Blackbird. We had no leadership, nothing. If the guy doesn't show up, the band doesn't get paid.

MORGAN: If Elvis doesn't show up, the Sweet Inspirations don't go on in his place! No one gives a shit about the Sweet Inspirations! The Sweet Inspirations don't exist without Elvis! They are his back-up singers! That's all they will ever be!

LADY JANE: I thought the Jordanaires were his back-up singers.

MORGAN: In the Fifties! In the Seventies, it was the Sweet Inspirations!

THOMPSON: Actually, in the seventies, it was both!

MORGAN: What do you know about it?

THOMPSON: What do you know about it? You're a relic from the sixties! You don't know from Elvis! Your idols are all, what, Jim Morrison, Arte Johnson, and Charlie Manson!

MORGAN: I grew up with Elvis! With Elvis and *Superman* and *Howdy Doody* and Sputnik and T V dinners! Who are your idols, Thompson? Fucking

Prince? Magnum P I? Mister T? Why did you try to storm the Bastille?

THOMPSON: Someone had to do something!

MORGAN: You had to do something? It's not your place to do anything, Thompson, not unless Blackbird tells you to! If you step outta that place, then you fuck up the machine!

THOMPSON: Look, I'm just here, like everyone else! Do you see me fucking up the machine?

MORGAN: What I see, Thompson, is you being Mister Gloomy. You've been here, ever since Blackbird came in the room, moping around here saying, "well, maybe, I dunno, I'm committed, maybe, so so", you were all ready to be Mister Vive La France, Mister Throw-Yourself-Into-The-Fire, Mister Rebel-Without-A-Brain, and our leader comes in the room, and suddenly you're Mister Well-I-Dunno-Maybe-So-So! Let me ask you a question, Mister I'm-Not-So-Sure-Negative-Attitude! Mister Doubting Thompson! Is Elvis back? Is Elvis in this room? DO YOU HAVE FAITH IN ELVIS?

THOMPSON: I have faith in Blackbird.

MORGAN: Do you? Do you really? What are you, the fucking missing link? We have to wait around for you to catch up? We're ready! I'm with Blackbird, Lady Jane is with Blackbird, Blackbird is with Blackbird, Clovis is here, you don't see him complaining! In fact, Clovis, at this point, is more committed to this project than you are!

THOMPSON: Morgan, you should be committed!

MORGAN: All Blackbird needs is time! And you won't give it to him! I'm happy just to hand him his guitar. Why isn't that enough for you? Something is really wrong here, Thompson! Really wrong!

THOMPSON: Wrong? What's wrong? Why are you so convinced that something's got to be wrong? Why are you so suspicious?

MORGAN: Suspicious? You're damn straight I'm suspicious! You'd have to have a fucking bullet in your brain not to be suspicious of the way you've been acting since Blackbird came back! Clovis is the only one in the room who isn't suspicious!

THOMPSON: What's with you anyway, Morgan? Why are you giving me this shit? I haven't done anything wrong have I?

MORGAN: *(Slowly)* Not that we know of.

THOMPSON: What's that supposed to mean?

MORGAN: Just this, Thompson! Just this! We have a problem. We have got a mighty fucking big problem. Someone is a traitor!

THOMPSON: You are really getting paranoid, Morgan!

MORGAN: It's true! Someone is a traitor! Who? Can you tell me that?

THOMPSON: I can't tell you that.

MORGAN: Is it you?

THOMPSON: Do you think it is?

MORGAN: I don't know! That's why I ask!

LADY JANE: Morgan—what the hell?

MORGAN: Lady Jane, we've got to figure this thing out! We can't do shit if we've got a traitor in our midst!

LADY JANE: Morgan, the traitor might not be in our midst!

MORGAN: But what if he is, Jane? That's the crucial question! What if he is?

LADY JANE: Don't you think we should let Blackbird figure that out?

(Beat)

MORGAN: All right. All right. We'll let Blackbird figure it out. *(To* BLACKBIRD:*)* Blackbird? What do you think? What do you think is at the root of Thompson's oh-so-questionable behavior? You're back, Blackbird. You are back. I'm happy. Jane's excited. Clovis hasn't changed a bit. But Thompson! Thompson is another story!

(Pause)

BLACKBIRD: Morgan?

MORGAN: Yes?

BLACKBIRD: Are you sincerely happy?

MORGAN: Me? I'm joyous! I'm obsessed! I'm redundant...with joy! I am with you! Jane is with you! What's wrong with Thompson?

BLACKBIRD: What do you think?

MORGAN: What do I think? What do I think? O K. I think the reason that the cops haven't shown up is because the person who tipped them off didn't want to destroy our organization—he wanted to *take over* our organization. He wanted to overthrow Elvis is a coup d'etat by proxy. I think that's what happened here. Little Elvis is trying to take over from Big Elvis. *(Beat)* You're Big Elvis.

BLACKBIRD: And Thompson's Little Elvis?

MORGAN: Well... That's the question, isn't it?

(Beat)

BLACKBIRD: Pretty strong stuff, Morgan.

MORGAN: *(Not so sure anymore)* Well, it's just a theory.

BLACKBIRD: Let's test out another theory. What about Jane?

MORGAN: What?

BLACKBIRD: Let's redirect the energy here. What makes Jane so free from suspicion?

MORGAN: Jane wouldn't betray us.

BLACKBIRD: Wouldn't she?

MORGAN: It doesn't make any sense for Jane to betray us.

BLACKBIRD: You don't think so.

MORGAN: I know so!

BLACKBIRD: Do you know that for a fact?

MORGAN: I...I strongly believe it with all of my heart.

BLACKBIRD: Your heart?

MORGAN: Yes.

BLACKBIRD: We should trust your heart?

MORGAN: Well—

BLACKBIRD: Your gut? Your instincts?

MORGAN: I'm not an expert or anything—

BLACKBIRD: Ask her.

MORGAN: What?

BLACKBIRD: Ask Jane if she betrayed us.

(Beat)

MORGAN: Jane?

LADY JANE: Yes, Morgan?

MORGAN: Did you betray us, Jane?

LADY JANE: No, Morgan. I didn't.

MORGAN: Good. *(To BLACKBIRD:)* She didn't betray us.

BLACKBIRD: How do you know?

MORGAN: She told me?

BLACKBIRD: And you think you can trust her?

MORGAN: Of course.

BLACKBIRD: Why?

MORGAN: Because...I just do.

BLACKBIRD: Pretty trusting, aren't you?

MORGAN: Of Lady Jane? Sure.

BLACKBIRD: Well, what about you, Morgan?

MORGAN: What? What about me?

BLACKBIRD: Let's examine your behavior for a moment.

MORGAN: What's wrong with my behavior?

BLACKBIRD: You ran, Morgan. When I found you, you were running away from the bank. Not into the bank. Away from it.

MORGAN: Yeah, but...

BLACKBIRD: You were supposed to be inside the bank, weren't you?

MORGAN: I was...

BLACKBIRD: You left your post, Morgan. That's a treasonous offense. Punishable by death.

MORGAN: But—

BLACKBIRD: But what, Morgan? Would you like us to overlook your little *faux pas*? What kind of an organization would we be if we did that?

MORGAN: But, Blackbird—!

BLACKBIRD: Desertion, Morgan. You deserted. You abandoned your comrades in the heat of battle.

MORGAN: Piñero sounded the retreat!

BLACKBIRD: So you say, Morgan. So you say.

MORGAN: You can't possibly think—

BLACKBIRD: I think that you ran, Morgan. You ran. And now you're trying to put the blame on Thompson.

MORGAN: I had no choice!

BLACKBIRD: No choice but to blame your comrade?

MORGAN: No choice but to *run*!

BLACKBIRD: So you say.

MORGAN: It was hopeless!

BLACKBIRD: So you say.

MORGAN: You weren't even there!

(Pause)

BLACKBIRD: What? What did you say?

MORGAN: Nothing.

BLACKBIRD: What did you say, Morgan?

MORGAN: Nothing.

BLACKBIRD: WHAT DID YOU SAY?

MORGAN: You weren't there, Blackbird. You weren't. You saved my ass across the street, but you never made it to the bank like you were supposed to. We were in there. Under fire. All alone. With no one to lead us. And you weren't there.

(Beat. For a moment, we think BLACKBIRD *might kill* MORGAN. *Then:)*

BLACKBIRD: A good point, Morgan. A very good point. I never even showed up. At least you made a heroic attempt. Or, at an rate, an attempt. Where was I, Morgan? Where was I?

MORGAN: You were on your way. You'd been detained.

BLACKBIRD: So I say.

MORGAN: I believe you.

BLACKBIRD: I could be lying.

MORGAN: You wouldn't lie.

BLACKBIRD: I wouldn't?

MORGAN: No.

BLACKBIRD: I might.

MORGAN: Never!

BLACKBIRD: I lied to the cops.

MORGAN: That's different! You wouldn't betray us!

BLACKBIRD: How do you know that?

MORGAN: I know! I just do!

BLACKBIRD: But you don't. You don't really. Do you?

(Beat)

MORGAN: No. Not really.

(Beat)

THOMPSON: It doesn't matter. It doesn't matter who the traitor is.

MORGAN: What are you talking about? Of course it matters.

THOMPSON: Why?

MORGAN: What?

THOMPSON: Why does it matter?

MORGAN: Because...we have to protect what remains of the organization!

THOMPSON: Nothing remains of the organization.

MORGAN: There's still us.

THOMPSON: Why does it matter what happens to us?

MORGAN: What?

THOMPSON: Give me a reason why.

(Beat)

MORGAN: *(To* BLACKBIRD*)* Blackbird? C'mon, Blackbird, help me out here. Give me a reason...for Thompson! One word, Blackbird. That's all we need here. One word.

*(*BLACKBIRD *says nothing.)*

(Pause)

MORGAN: Jesus Christ, is it over?

THOMPSON: Morgan, I...

MORGAN: I can't believe that.

THOMPSON: Well, I mean...

MORGAN: Is it?

THOMPSON: It depends...

MORGAN: Is it time to give up?

THOMPSON: I don't...

MORGAN: Is it time to go home?

THOMPSON: It's not exactly...

MORGAN: Is it time to roll over and die?

THOMPSON: Not necessarily.

MORGAN: But maybe?

THOMPSON: Maybe.

MORGAN: Possibly?

THOMPSON: Possibly.

MORGAN: Conceivably?

THOMPSON: Conceivably.

LADY JANE: No! *(Silence)* No. It's not over. It's never over. Not until the last gasp. Don't you tell me that. Don't you dare tell me that. *(Beat)* Why do you think we struggle? Why do we fight? If you think we do all this just to win, to rack up points, like this is some game, the politically radical Olympics, then you're wrong. As long as there is struggle, there is hope. As long as there is hope, there is meaning. And creating meaning, in the lives of others as well ourselves is the most noble thing a human can do.

(Beat)

BLACKBIRD: Well, I'm really beginning to wonder what's happened to us. What's become of our spirit? Our resolution? Why are we floating around in the dark?

LADY JANE: Blackbird...we've put ourselves in your hands.

BLACKBIRD: Was that wise?

LADY JANE: You told us our past lives are over. The person we were before we met you is dead. Forget who that person was. Never speak the names of the people or the places of that life. You re-christened us. You picked new names for us. So we would be reborn. We came to you, new and naked like babies. To start our lives again from ground zero. From year zero. We put ourselves completely in your hands. We've done nothing you haven't asked us to, Blackbird. You came to us, Blackbird. You came to us and you told us you had something for us to do. Something worthwhile. You gave us all a reason to struggle. A reason to fight. You're our leader, Blackbird. You told us you could lead us and we offered to follow you. Isn't that the way you want it? Isn't that why we are all here?

(Silence)

BLACKBIRD: Morgan, where were you born?

MORGAN: What?

BLACKBIRD: Where were you born?

MORGAN: I'm not supposed to give out that kind of information.

BLACKBIRD: Where were you born, Morgan?

MORGAN: Somewhere.

LADY JANE: Blackbird, you told us never again to speak of our former lives. We started again with you. Naked like newborns.

BLACKBIRD: A good point. Get undressed.

THOMPSON: What?

BLACKBIRD: Come to me. New and naked. To be reborn. Again. *(Beat)* DO AS I SAY! GET UNDRESSED! NOW!

(Beat. They all strip naked, except BLACKBIRD *and* CLOVIS. *When they are naked,* BLACKBIRD *regards them.)*

BLACKBIRD: Morgan...do you know where you were born?

MORGAN: Yes.

BLACKBIRD: Where?

MORGAN: Somewhere.

BLACKBIRD: Where was that?

MORGAN: Someplace else.

LADY JANE: Don't do this, Blackbird.

BLACKBIRD: What state?

MORGAN: The United States.

BLACKBIRD: Which one?

MORGAN: All of them.

BLACKBIRD: It can't have been all of them.

MORGAN: It was.

BLACKBIRD: It can't.

MORGAN: It was.

BLACKBIRD: Which one?

MORGAN: One of them.

LADY JANE: Why are you doing this, Blackbird?

BLACKBIRD: Which one was that?

MORGAN: My favorite one.

BLACKBIRD: Which one was that?

MORGAN: The one where I was born.

BLACKBIRD: What was its name?

MORGAN: Its name?

BLACKBIRD: Its name.

MORGAN: Its name is the same name as the name of the state in which I was born.

BLACKBIRD: And what was that?

MORGAN: The name of my favorite state.

LADY JANE: Blackbird!

BLACKBIRD: And what was that name?

MORGAN: Its own name.

BLACKBIRD: Its own name different from any other name?

MORGAN: Yes.

BLACKBIRD: How so?

MORGAN: How so how?

BLACKBIRD: Different in what way? What distinguishes your home state's name from any other state's name?

MORGAN: It was its own name. Its own personal name that no one else had. No one could touch its name, because it was its own and no one else's. Its own private property. It didn't need to announce it. It didn't need to make a big deal of it. There were no banners or road signs proclaiming it. Even our license plates had no slogan. Its name was its name and everyone knew that and everyone respected that. So it didn't need to be said.

(Beat)

BLACKBIRD: Funny little state you come from.

MORGAN: Best in the Union.

BLACKBIRD: Morgan...where were you born?

(Beat)

MORGAN: Here.

BLACKBIRD: When?

MORGAN: Just now.

(Beat)

BLACKBIRD: What are your parents' names, Thompson?

THOMPSON: What?

BLACKBIRD: Your parents' names?

THOMPSON: Why?

BLACKBIRD: Just curious.

THOMPSON: Why?

BLACKBIRD: No reason.

THOMPSON: It doesn't really matter, does it?

BLACKBIRD: No. Not really.

THOMPSON: Then why ask?

BLACKBIRD: No reason. Why don't you want to tell me?

LADY JANE: Blackbird!

THOMPSON: I don't *not* want to tell you.

BLACKBIRD: Then why won't you tell me?

THOMPSON: I didn't say I wouldn't tell you.

BLACKBIRD: Then tell me.

LADY JANE: Blackbird, stop it!

THOMPSON: I just wanted to know the reason why you wanted to know.

BLACKBIRD: So, tell me.

LADY JANE: Please.

THOMPSON: I wanted to know if it was merely an idle question or if it had some significance.

BLACKBIRD: Do you know the names of your parents?

THOMPSON: Of course I do.

BLACKBIRD: I mean, not everyone has parents.

THOMPSON: What's that supposed to mean?

BLACKBIRD: Some people are orphans.

THOMPSON: I'm not.

BLACKBIRD: Good. So what are the names of your parents?

LADY JANE: Blackbird…

THOMPSON: I'm not telling.

BLACKBIRD: Is there something you want to hide, Thompson? Some dark family secret? Some skeletons in your closet? Is there a curse on your family name?

THOMPSON: It's none of your damn business!

BLACKBIRD: Now we get to the heart of the matter.

THOMPSON: Yes we do.

BLACKBIRD: You don't want to tell me.

THOMPSON: No.

BLACKBIRD: I have no right to inquire.

LADY JANE: Well, do you?

THOMPSON: No.

BLACKBIRD: Or perhaps you don't know.

THOMPSON: Of course I know!

BLACKBIRD: Do you? Do you even know your own name, Thompson?

THOMPSON: What?

BLACKBIRD: First name, last name, middle name? We know you only as "Thompson".

THOMPSON: That's because that's the name you gave me. You rechristened us all.

BLACKBIRD: What is your full name, Thompson?

THOMPSON: You told me never to speak it again.

BLACKBIRD: You don't know, do you? *(Silence)* I don't suppose you remember the name of your home state, either? *(Silence)* I didn't think so. *(To* MORGAN:*)* You can't tell me your full name, can you, Morgan? *(Silence)* No? *(Silence)* Can't or won't? *(Silence. To* THOMPSON:*)* Thompson...what are your parents names?

(Beat)

THOMPSON: Flynt. Blackbird Flynt. He is my mother and my father. I have no other parents. He is the only one. I sprang from his forehead, fully grown, and rode to shore on the crest of a wave.

BLACKBIRD: That's what we like to hear. *(To* LADY JANE:*)* How about you, Jane? *(He goes to* LADY JANE *and violently pulls back her hair.)* What have you got to share with me? *(Silence)* Do you even know where we are, Jane? *(Silence. He grips her hair, tighter.)* Do you know what state it is that we are in now, Lady Jane?

(Silence. BLACKBIRD *leaves* LADY JANE, *letting go of her hair. She collapses. Beat)*

BLACKBIRD: What do you want, Jane?

LADY JANE: What do you mean?

BLACKBIRD: What do you want out of life?

LADY JANE: What, like, kids and a house and vacations in the Dells?

BLACKBIRD: Is that what you want?

LADY JANE: No. I don't know. Maybe. After the revolution.

BLACKBIRD: What does the revolution bring about? In your mind?

*(*LADY JANE *thinks, then rises, and composes herself.)*

LADY JANE: Well. An end to poverty. A redistribution of wealth. An end to the reification of labor.

BLACKBIRD: You know your Marx.

LADY JANE: I read a lot in the commune.

BLACKBIRD: What else?

*(*LADY JANE *speaks with increasing confidence.)*

LADY JANE: An end to racism. An end to sexism. An end to imperialist aggression.

BLACKBIRD: What else?

*(*BLACKBIRD *steps towards* LADY JANE, *but she moves away. They begin to stalk and circle one another as they speak. She keeps a certain distance from him, not so much in fear, but to assert some modicum of control.)*

LADY JANE: An increase in human dignity. A rise in social justice.

BLACKBIRD: More.

LADY JANE: A society based on communal effort rather than profit and exploitation.

BLACKBIRD: More.

LADY JANE: An end to violence. An end to abuse.

BLACKBIRD: What else?

LADY JANE: National liberation.

BLACKBIRD: More.

LADY JANE: A return to the peoples of the world the wealth created by their labor. The destruction of U S military and economic imperialism and the achievement of a classless world. An end to white-skin privilege.

BLACKBIRD: Don't bore me with tired New Left clichés! Go deeper!

LADY JANE: Freedom of speech, freedom of worship, freedom from want, freedom from fear!

BLACKBIRD: Roosevelt's four freedoms?

LADY JANE: They're good freedoms.

BLACKBIRD: What else?

LADY JANE: Unity.

BLACKBIRD: More!

LADY JANE: Self-determination.

BLACKBIRD: More!

LADY JANE: Collective work and responsibility.

BLACKBIRD: More!

LADY JANE: Cooperative economics.

BLACKBIRD: More!

LADY JANE: An end to the social dysfunction and degradation of everyday life inflcited by advanced capitalism!

BLACKBIRD: More!

LADY JANE: Purpose. Creativity. Faith.

BLACKBIRD: Faith in what?

(Beat)

LADY JANE: I don't know.

BLACKBIRD: Faith in what? God?

LADY JANE: Maybe.

BLACKBIRD: Humankind?

LADY JANE: Maybe.

BLACKBIRD: Faith in what?

(Beat)

(They stand still.)

LADY JANE: In you, Blackbird. Faith in you. *(Silence. To* BLACKBIRD:*)* Your turn, now.

BLACKBIRD: Excuse me?

LADY JANE: None of us actually knows anything about you. What's your pedigree? Your anarcho-communal revolutionary vanguardian credentials? S D S? Citizens' Commission to Investigate the F B I? Youth International Party? Black Liberation Army? Prairie Fire Organizing Committee? Weather Underground? Symbionese Liberation Army? Baader-Meinhof Gang? May 19th Communist Organization? Red diaper baby? Where do you come from? Or did you burst fully formed from Abbie Hoffman's cranium? Or maybe Joe Strummer's left testicle? Who the hell are *you*?

(Silence)

BLACKBIRD: Get dressed, all of you. You look ridiculous.

(Silence, as they all get dressed.)

(Suddenly, THOMPSON *runs to* BLACKBIRD *with his fist raised to hit him. But when he gets to him, he can't do it. He freezes and, in frustration, throws himself to the wall, as if plastered to it.)*

THOMPSON: Give us a sign, Blackbird! Lead us out of here!

BLACKBIRD: I can't take responsibility for your lives if you can't. I can't lead you out of the desert if you can't keep up.

THOMPSON: Everyone is dead! All our hopes are shattered! Our lives up in smoke! We don't need a Messiah! We just need a little help! A simple plan of action! Help us forge ourselves a new direction! The old one points to nowhere!

BLACKBIRD: I can't give you any easy answers, Thompson. Easy answers are hollow ones. If that's what you want, write your congressman.

THOMPSON: WE DON'T NEED CONGRESSMEN! THAT'S THE WHOLE POINT OF WHAT WE'RE DOING! THAT SENATORS AND CONGRESSMEN AND PRESIDENTS ARE OUTDATED! THEY HAVE CEASED TO SERVE ANY TRUE FUNCTION, THEY NO LONGER ADDRESS THE NEEDS OF THE PEOPLE! THEY CANNOT HELP US! SENATORS SUCK! THEY DO NO GOOD! ARE YOU ONE OF THEM, BLACKBIRD? ARE YOU?

(Beat)

BLACKBIRD: What did you call me? Did you call me a senator? Is that what you called me? Get down off that wall, mister.

THOMPSON: I CAN'T I'M STUCK! SO THERE!

(Beat)

MORGAN: Get off the wall, Thompson.

LADY JANE: Yes. Please.

THOMPSON: No! I'm stuck here and here I'll stay!

LADY JANE: Please, Thompson. It would be so much easier.

(Beat. THOMPSON *slowly relaxes and peels himself off the wall.)*

(Beat)

BLACKBIRD: I'm sorry I snapped at you, Thompson.

*(*THOMPSON *does not answer or look* BLACKBIRD *in the eye. He sits in a seat and lights a cigarette.)*

BLACKBIRD: May I have one of those?

*(*THOMPSON *does not offer* BLACKBIRD *one.* BLACKBIRD *does not persist.)*

BLACKBIRD: There's some horrible stench in the air. Like...Roquefort.

(Silence)

MORGAN: Let's steal a car. Let's take a drive.

LADY JANE: Where to?

MORGAN: Anywhere. To the beach. We'll go to the beach and swim. Make a big bonfire. Drink. Have a clambake. Play volleyball. Skinny dip. I don't know. Anything. As long as we do it on the beach.

LADY JANE: I like the beach.

THOMPSON: I prefer Las Vegas.

MORGAN: You can't. You're a revolutionary.

THOMPSON: Oh. Right.

BLACKBIRD: *(Looking off into the distance in his mind's eye:)* You like cars. You like to drive. You used to drive all the time. Before you moved to the city. The windy city.

MORGAN: When did I move to the windy city?

LADY JANE: Shhh. He's not talking about you.

MORGAN: Whose he talking about, then?

BLACKBIRD: Born in the southern plains. Walked barefoot to school. Had a secret swimming hole. Swam in the cool waters in the afternoon. Then up north to the windy city. Cold. Big. Noisy. Windy. You buy a leather jacket, a motorcycle jacket, to keep warm and to look cool. You hang out with the wrong crowd. The city is big, and you are lonely. You start to steal cars. At first it's a game. You drive to the outskirts of town and throw stones at the abandoned factory's windows. Then it becomes a business. You steal cars and strip them down. You always have money. For drugs, sex, records. You're one of the best car thieves in the city and everybody knows it, but no one can catch you. Any car you want, you can steal. Then it becomes an obsession. You can't stop stealing cars. The money doesn't matter any more. It's the act of car theft that does. You can't help it. You see a car, you have to steal it. You steal so many cars you can't possibly strip them all. It gets so bad that you empty entire parking lots in one fell swoop. Just one car after another. Drive them a block away, park, then back for another. People come out of the buildings at five o'clock and their cars are gone. Not actually stolen, really. Just moved. Something's in your blood now. It's an art form. The aesthetics of auto theft. You live for auto theft. You live car to car. You lose yourself. You lose your name. You lose your identity. You are the Kid Who Steals Cars. Nothing more.

Then the day comes when you steal your last car. The very last one. The last car of a day full of cars. The last car of a parking lot full of cars. Four forty-five and you're running out of time. Soon the working day will be over and everyone will leave the surrounding buildings, heading for the parking lot, car keys in hand. You can't seem to get this last one started. It's just an old beat up Ford, and the damn thing won't start. Four fifty-five. Time's running out on you fast. But you can't leave without this one. It's the most important of all. You realize it's the last one. The last one of all time. You see some old dude in a gray suit step out of a building across the street. He stops. He looks towards you. His face turns white. He starts yelling and running at you. This is it? The end of the Car Theft Kid?

The motor suddenly coughs and sputters and sparks to life. You back it out at sixty miles an hour and leave the guy in the suit jumping up and down and swearing at you. You race through the city. You're having fun now. Real fun. You've never gone this fast in the city before. You know it's stupid. You don't care. You're having fun. The street lights whiz by. The buildings turn into one great big gray mass. People disappear. Buildings melt into houses. Houses into trees. Trees into fields. You realize you're on the highway. Going a hundred miles an hour. Not bad for an old beat up Ford. But this isn't just any old beat up Ford. This is the quintessential old beat up Ford. The old beat up Ford to end all old beat up Fords. The old beat up Ford of the century. The old beat up Ford that ate Manhattan. This is destiny, kid. Don't look back now. Just keep on driving.

Day turns into night and night into day. You travel more miles than you can count. You don't even need to stop for gas. This is the old beat up Ford of the Century, and it'll carry you on through to where you wanna go. You pass by rundown shacks with rotting roofs and a kid playing in the dirt outside. You pass by abandoned farmhouses. You pass by mountains and lakes. Amber waves of grain. Then you come alongside of an old train a half a mile long. Creeping forward at twenty-five miles an hour. Blocking off entire sections of countryside. Splitting the country in two for a half a mile. For ten minutes, no way to get from one side to another, because there's this great big moving wall between you and the other side. You stop the car. You start to panic. You start to scream. Where is this, Berlin? Why is there a wall between me and the rest of the country? Why is there an Iron

Curtain in the middle of the United States? This is not Eastern Europe! This is America! The Land of the Free! The Home of the Brave! There are no Iron Curtains in America! Since when have there been Iron Curtains in America? *(Beat)* You watch as the train passes you and goes on down the track, getting smaller and smaller as it chugs along. Goddamn snail of a train. You gather yourself and you get back in the car. You wipe the sweat from your brow. You start the car, the engine turns over, and you take off. You want to catch up to that train. Catch up to it and pass it. Make it eat your dust. You speed on ahead. The train has a good head start, so you floor it. You're making tracks now. The old beat up Ford of the Century is coming through. Then up ahead you see a railroad crossing. You realize that this lumbering dinosaur train has shifted direction. It's going to pass right in front of you unless you get there first. You can make it, you say to yourself. You must be going a hundred and twenty, easy. You see the train ahead to the right, chugging along, steam pouring from its stack. You wonder why, with all that steam, it still goes so slowly. The bells at the crossing start to ring, the lights start to flash, and the arm starts to come down. But you'll make it. You're gaining. You look back at the train. You see the gray steam framed against the clear blue sky. You look back at the crossing. The arm is down now. But that's O K. You'll smash right on through and out the other side. You notice the faded red stripes on the cracked white wood. You look back at the Iron Curtain. It's almost at the crossing now, spitting steam, whistle blowing, it's almost on top of you now. You're not going to make it. You're not going to make it.

You slam on the brakes and jerk the wheel to the left. The car screeches a painful sound that like two hawks fighting. You do a one-eighty plus. The train's horn blares and the tone sounds just like some Goddamn school teacher chewing you out, with the entire class laughing at you to boot. The back end of your car smashes through the gate and stops three inches from the tracks. You sit there, staring in front of you, your back to the train, watching the shadow of the cars as they pass. Catching glimpses of the train in your rear view mirror. There she goes. The Iron Curtain Express. Chugging along at its leisure. Not a care in the Goddamn world. A half mile of Iron Curtain passes behind you, casting its shadow over your car for twenty minutes. For twenty minutes you sit there, too angry to look back. Beaten by a broken down old steam engine train. A relic of the nineteenth century. Laughing at you. A relic of the twentieth century. Cut off from the rest of the country twice in one day by the same portable Berlin wall.

The train passes and you sit there until you can't even hear it chugging along any more. Then you turn the car around and head east as fast as you possibly can.

(Silence)

CLOVIS: HAPPY NEW YEAR!

BLACKBIRD: He talks.

THOMPSON: He does that sometimes.

CLOVIS: Welcome home, boys…fine mess we have here…hmm…so glad to have…you back…oh boy…I just got a new car…

BLACKBIRD: What kind of car?

CLOVIS: A purple…car…convertible…a purple convertible car…convertible into…what? …Into another car just like it, faster than you can say Blackbird Flynt…or is it Finch?

BLACKBIRD: Flynt. It's Flynt.

CLOVIS: So glad to hear that…you're coming home… after all these years mister . . mister…mister…

BLACKBIRD: Flynt. Blackbird Flynt.

CLOVIS: Good… *(His eyes suddenly open for the first time.)* Oh, my God! Several billion people! Not one of them true! It's astounding! The figures are astounding! The planet Earth spins around so fast it could make you puke! And it does! Oh boy! Everywhere you go, the figures are astounding! People walking down the street, up one side and down another and never knowing what they're doing! Where they're going! Why they're doing it! It's astounding! The figures are astounding…

BLACKBIRD: Clovis?

CLOVIS: You interrupted me…

BLACKBIRD: Sorry.

CLOVIS: That's all right. I talk a lot. It's my vocation. I read the bible aloud to illegitimate children of God. There is much misery in the world, my son. The figures are astounding. What can I do for you, my son?

(Beat)

BLACKBIRD: I want to kick the world in the groin, Father. Kick it in the groin and scream in its ear. If I can do that much, so that the memory of the pain will not go away, then I will be happy. I must leave a stain upon the universe before I leave it. I cannot live in its excrement and not throw some back in its face. I cannot live this way any longer. Father. That I cannot do.

CLOVIS: Worthy sentiments, my son…hang on…for a while…please…give…generously… *(He drifts back into restless sleep.)*

(Beat)

LADY JANE: So, Blackbird. Where do we go from here?

(Pause)

BLACKBIRD: I'll show you. *(He goes to the guns on the table and picks one up.)*

LADY JANE: What are you getting at, Blackbird?

BLACKBIRD: Something very simple.

LADY JANE: Why?

BLACKBIRD: Because it is the only way.

LADY JANE: Why?

BLACKBIRD: This way we can be something more than what we are. We can transcend ourselves. We can become symbols of strength and courage and selfless sacrifice. We will become heroes of the modern age. *(Beat)* It will be the perfect ending. We will have lived and died in perfect accordance with our ideals. And we will be remembered and admired for it. We can, in this way, inspire others much more effectively than anything else it is within our power to achieve. Our true goal will be fulfilled. We shall move others to act, to rise up and say "No!". We shall live on in the revolution that our actions and our memory shall perpetuate. We will succeed. Will we create meaning. It is the most noble thing a person can do.

(Pause)

MORGAN: Oh my God…

BLACKBIRD: *(Offering him a gun)* Every revolution needs its martyrs, Morgan. This is your chance. Are you ready to make the supreme sacrifice? Who is with me? *(He turns to* THOMPSON *offering him a gun.)* Thompson? You can't sit on your ass and wait for revolution, Thompson. You know that. *(Beat)* Do you want me to tell you what to do?

THOMPSON: Yes.

BLACKBIRD: Good. *(He turns to* LADY JANE*, offering her a gun.)* Jane? *(Beat)* It's easy, Jane. It is really very, very easy.

LADY JANE: What about Clovis?

BLACKBIRD: Clovis will tell our story.

LADY JANE: He's got a bullet in his brain.

THOMPSON: I thought you said—

LADY JANE: Shut up.

BLACKBIRD: Clovis will recover. He will recover and he will burn our corpses on a pyre and he will scatter our ashes and he will tell our story and he will become a prophet and inspire the revolution. A revolution that will rise up and overthrow the fascist order and bring about peace and social and economic justice. Jane—do you have faith in me?

LADY JANE: I do.

BLACKBIRD: Then trust me. The Revolution is not dead as long as there are people willing to die for it, Jane. *(Beat)* What are you without me, Jane? Do you know?

LADY JANE: *(Taking the gun)* Yes.

BLACKBIRD: I knew you did.

(Silence. Then, they all slowly move into position. BLACKBIRD *and* LADY JANE *facing each other,* MORGAN *and* THOMPSON *facing each other, each of the four as points on a circle.)*

BLACKBIRD: Ready?

LADY JANE: Ready.

MORGAN: Ready.

THOMPSON: Ready.

(They raise their pistols.)

BLACKBIRD: Good-bye, Morgan. Good-bye, Thompson. Good-bye, Jane.

MORGAN: Good-bye, Thompson. Good-bye, Jane. Good-bye, Blackbird.

THOMPSON: Good-bye, Morgan. Good-bye, Jane. Good-bye, Blackbird.

LADY JANE: Good-bye, Morgan. Good-bye, Thompson. Good-bye, Blackbird.

(Beat)

BLACKBIRD: On three.

(They all aim at the person opposite them.)

BLACKBIRD: One. Two. Three.

(All pull their trigger except for LADY JANE. *All three hammers click against an empty barrel. They all freeze. Beat.)*

THOMPSON: Blackbird? I think you forgot to load the pistols.

BLACKBIRD: Jane still hasn't fired hers. *(Beat)* Jane? Pull the trigger. Now. *(Beat)* Please?

(Slowly, LADY JANE *points her pistol not at* BLACKBIRD, *but at the ceiling and fires. This time, the gun goes off. Long pause as they all stare at each other, immobile, guns still raised.)*

*(*CLOVIS *suddenly springs awake again with a gasp or a sharp intake of air, some kind of noise, not too loud, but noticeable, sitting up, wide-eyed.)*

(Everyone turns to look at CLOVIS.*)*

(Blackout)

(Curtain)

END OF PLAY

Made in the USA
Lexington, KY
30 April 2019